Connecting Top Managers

Developing Executive Teams for Business Success

Jim Taylor
Lisa Haneberg

Vice President, Publisher: Tim Moore
Associate Publisher and Director of Marketing: Amy Neidlinger
Executive Editor: Jeanne Glasser
Editorial Assistant: Pamela Boland
Development Editor: Russ Hall
Operations Manager: Gina Kanouse
Senior Marketing Manager: Julie Phifer
Publicity Manager: Laura Czaja
Assistant Marketing Manager: Megan Colvin
Cover Designer: Chuti Prasertsith
Managing Editor: Kristy Hart
Project Editor: Anne Goebel
Copy Editor: Language Logistics, LLC
Proofreader: Kathy Ruiz
Indexer: Lisa Stumpf
Compositor: Nonie Ratcliff
Manufacturing Buyer: Dan Uhrig

© 2011 by MPI Consulting
Publishing as FT Press
Upper Saddle River, New Jersey 07458

FT Press offers excellent discounts on this book when ordered in quantity for bulk purchases
or special sales. For more information, please contact U.S. Corporate and Government Sales,
1-800-382-3419, corpsales@pearsontechgroup.com. For sales outside the U.S., please contact
International Sales at international@pearson.com.

Printed in the United States of America

First Printing December 2010

Pearson Education LTD.
Pearson Education Australia PTY, Limited.
Pearson Education Singapore, Pte. Ltd.
Pearson Education Asia, Ltd.
Pearson Education Canada, Ltd.
Pearson Educación de Mexico, S.A. de C.V.
Pearson Education—Japan
Pearson Education Malaysia, Pte. Ltd.

Library of Congress Cataloging-in-Publication Data:

Taylor, Jim, 1949-
  Connecting top managers : developing executive teams for business success / Jim Taylor, Lisa
Haneberg. -- 1st ed.
    p. cm
  Includes bibliographical references and index.
  ISBN 978-0-13-707156-2 (hardback : alk. paper) 1. Leadership. 2. Business ethics. 3.
Teams in the workplace. 4. Success in business. I. Haneberg, Lisa. II. Title.
  HD57.7.T385 2011
  658.4'022--dc22
                              2010045726

ISBN-10: 0-13-707156-6
ISBN-13: 978-0-13-707156-2

Contents

Foreword

I recently had the honor of being inducted into the Pro Football Hall of Fame and spent some time reflecting on my 52-year career as a player and coach. I thought about the successes of which I was most proud, the failures that still sting, and the lessons I have learned about teams and participating in the process of leading.

One lesson is that it's all about the team. The ultimate team sport is football. Everyone must work together and accept his role for the group to succeed. Everyone is needed; no one is essential. All must function as a unit to allow the desired victorious results.

The most skilled and talented team often does not win. And we have seen underdog teams rise to glory fueled seemingly on a collective will, love, or something else more powerful. Why does this happen? It happens because effort and execution—our physical game—is deeply linked to and supported by our mental game, or how we are feeling about our team and our mission. The power of a unified group is a very real and tangible thing.

Great teams are connected to one another; each person is invested in the success of the other, as each one embraces their particular roles in the process of team building. All roles, even those in waiting, are critical. I can remember seasons when my team had a special quality and was a very strong unit of performance; watching them work together was the ultimate pleasure of coaching. I have also seen extremely talented teams underperform together because the spirit of unity was missing.

One of the most important lessons I have learned is that the power of great teams is not limited to the playing field and that the relationships are at the core of every team. The same dynamic has played out in my work as a player, coach, leader, friend, and father. Great relationships fuel results. Connection, cohesion, respect, and collaboration are some of the most important qualities of any team, whether they are of athletic or business orientation.

Lisa Haneberg and my friend Jim Taylor have done an outstanding job capturing the essential lessons of great leadership teamwork in this book. Their assertions that executives ought to be great team members are right on, and their methods and suggestions will help any leadership team improve their results.

Over the years, I have learned about the importance of the depth, strength, and openness of professional relationships. The best teams tap into their individual and collective talents to steer their performance for optimal results. It may seem mystical or esoteric, but it's not. Relationships are built through deliberate actions and intentions. This book will inspire your intentions and show you how to proactively build a stronger executive team. On the field and in the boardroom, who we are as leadership team members is a key factor in the formula for success.

—*Dick LeBeau, NFL Hall of Fame 2010*

Acknowledgments

We would like to thank our clients for providing the rich and helpful examples that we have presented throughout this book. While we have not named you here, you will know the story is yours, and we thank you for being a part of the book and learning experience. We would also like to thank our colleagues who offered their stories and blog posts, including Connie Kocher, Terry Starbucker, Wally Bock, and Dwayne Melancon. We would like to thank our agent Jeffrey Krames for being a great source of wisdom and ideas for how to shape this book and our editor at the FT Press, Jeanne Glasser, for believing in this work and for being such a joy to work with. We would also like to thank the teams that participated in our senior leadership team survey and focus group participants. And last but not least, we would like to thank our staff at MPI Consulting, especially Angie King and Nancy Sies, who helped us pull this book together.

From Jim:

I would like to thank Dick LeBeau for his friendship and inspiration. I value the closeness of our families, the role model you served with inspiring my two sons, your leadership skills, and your positive influence on so many leaders and players in the NFL. You deserve to be a member of the Hall of Fame (inducted in 2010).

I would also like to thank the thousands of senior leaders from California to Texas to Florida to Connecticut to Ohio who I have had had the opportunity to meet, get to know, and learn about their organizations in so many diverse industries, from health care to manufacturing to coal mines to food processing to telecommunications. I am thankful to have had the opportunity to consult with Fortune 100 companies, medium and small heart-run organizations, and many family-owned companies.

As a small town boy who came from a town of just 900 people and very humble roots, I am thankful everyday to have the privilege of leading an innovative, well-respected, boutique management consulting firm. I admire this company and the work we do. This book is really a culmination of decades of doing what I know and love.

And I would like to especially thank my wife, Myrna, and my sons, Ryan and Neil, for their support of me and my work.

From Lisa:

Like Jim, I am thankful to have had the opportunity to get to know and learn from some of the most talented leaders. And while there are too many to mention every one, I would like to acknowledge several leaders who inspired content in this book including Jerre Fuqua, Timo Shaw, Ronald Korenhof, Brenda Gumbs, Neil Winslow, Ralph Stayer, Mark Riley, Beth Hildreth, Bob Keyes, and Lisa Edwards.

I would also like to thank fellow thought leaders and bloggers who keep me on my toes and inspire me including John Kotter, Steve Farber, Marshall Goldsmith, David Ulrich, Mihaly Csikszentmihalyi, Tony Schwartz, Bill Strickland, Terry Starbucker, Wally Bock, Dwayne Melancon, Raj Setty, Dan Pink, Rosa Say, Tanmay Mora, Wayne Turmel, Phil Gerbyshak, Alexandra Levit, Jodee Bock, Todd Sattersten, and Tom Peters. Without you, the book would have been much more boring and unenlightened!

Introduction: A Pack of Top Dogs

Lisa was sitting with the CEO of a food manufacturer discussing the model for their senior leadership team. The CEO and his vice president of human resources had taken a stab at creating their model and had emailed it to Lisa the week before and asked for her input.

"I think what you have here is great, but it is incomplete," Lisa said. "You are missing half the model."

"Really, how so?" asked the CEO with great interest.

Lisa pulled a simple one-page diagram from a folder. "What you have defined is your expectations for what great functional leadership means to you and at this organization. What you have not yet addressed are your expectations for how your team ought to lead together or what senior leadership *team* excellence looks like and the impact you expect your team should have on steering this organization, results, culture, and the strength of the management function."

The CEO saw the power of the revised model immediately, and it changed his approach to how he and his team would lead together, and it expanded his definition of senior leadership team excellence.

This is a true story and one that we have seen played out with many leaders over the years. These experiences inspired us to write this book and share with you what we have learned about leadership teams and how to boost the positive impact they can have on organizations.

Many organizations use incomplete leadership models, which is not surprising because leaders often tend to focus on their functional

1

(or divisional) responsibilities. Most of their time is spent running the part of the business they have been hired to lead. Their financial rewards are likely tied to unit success, and the people in their unit are who they represent at leadership team meetings and during strategic planning sessions. Recruiting and hiring decisions are often based primarily on previous results as a group leader, and bigger and broader job opportunities are often offered to the leaders who have effectively managed their units.

And so it is not at all surprising to us that the other part of the leadership model, the part that we call leadership team excellence, is often overlooked. You might be thinking that this makes perfect sense. That 95% of a leader's time is spent running his or her function or unit, and therefore we should focus on, measure, and reward leaders based on what happens there. If departments and divisions don't perform well, organizations can't succeed.

We agree that functional success is critical *and* that it represents only half of the picture of excellence. Here are a few things we have learned that we hope will compel you to keep reading:

- Leadership teams, as a whole, create the culture and set the tone for how managers and employees work.
- One of the greatest predictors of whether a workforce will seek union representation and whether a union campaign will succeed is the connection and trust employees have established with the leadership team.
- Clashing styles within the leadership team have a strong, rippling, and negative effect on the entire organization.
- Although they are the most expensive in the organization in terms of payroll and opportunity costs, many leadership team meetings fail to produce satisfactory results.

Throughout this book, we explore these and many other ways that leaders, as a team, impact organizational success. We share examples, research, and actionable practices that you and your team members can use to enhance your results across several measures of excellence.

We believe in the 5/95 Rule. Five percent of your time—the approximately 100 hours per year that you spend together as a team—impacts 95% of the success of several organizational systems. If you can optimize this 5%, you will see positive returns in many areas including organizational culture, employee engagement and retention, productivity and results, and organizational agility. We have designed and organized this book to help leadership teams make the most of this precious 5%.

Who This Book Is For

We have written this book for leaders. Leaders are members of at least two teams—their functional or unit groups and their peer leadership teams. Our focus is on helping leaders and their team colleagues get better together. Members of middle management teams will also benefit from the recommendations we share, and we invite human resources, organization development, and training professionals to use this book to develop their leaders and leadership teams as well.

> *"The leaders who work most effectively, it seems to me, never say 'I.' And that's not because they have trained themselves not to say 'I.' They don't think 'I.' They think 'we'; they think 'team.' They understand their job to be to make the team function. They accept responsibility and don't sidestep it, but 'we' gets the credit.... This is what creates trust, what enables you to get the task done."[1]*
> —Peter Drucker

Who We Are

Jim Taylor and Lisa Haneberg work together at MPI Consulting, a boutique management consulting firm headquartered in Cincinnati, Ohio. Jim is the president and CEO of MPI Consulting and is a leading expert on what organizations can and should do to remain union-free. He has worked with over 300 leadership teams to help them build positive employee relations environments and has seen the impact that great and not-so-great senior teams can have on company culture, union vulnerability, and corporate success. Lisa is vice-president and leads the firm's organizational development practice. She is a nationally known thought leader in the areas of leadership, middle management, and organizational development. Both Jim and Lisa were successful leaders inside large organizations before becoming consultants.

How the Book Is Organized

Other than Chapter 1, "Executive Team Execution," which describes our model and lists our recommendations regarding how leadership teams ought to measure their success, the chapters can be read and used in any order. We have brought together our best thinking and the best practices from organizations and other thought leaders to give you compelling and specific ideas about leadership team excellence. We have also conducted focus groups and targeted surveys to augment and add color to the information.

Time Is Precious

We have designed this book to help leadership teams make the most of their time together. Rest assured that we do not suggest massive systems that take too many of your 100 hours together. We have selected best practices that make good use of that precious time.

We believe, and our work and research supports, that how leaders work together is as important as how well they lead their individual departments. The executives we have worked with over the last 36 years have been strong, smart, hardworking professionals promoted and praised based on their individual leadership and management capabilities and results. When they come together as a team, they are a pack of top dogs. The skills and practices that got them promoted may not be the same ones that are needed to be a great leadership team member.

What if your impact and success depends on how well you and your fellow leaders work *together*? We believe that it does and invite you to dive right into Chapter 1.

"Work can be one of the most joyful, most fulfilling aspects of life. Whether it will be or not depends on the actions we collectively take."[2]

—Mihaly Csikszentmihalyi

Endnotes

1. Peter Drucker, *Managing the Non-Profit Organization: Practices and Principles*, 18.

2. Mihaly Csikszentmihalyi, *Good Business: Leadership, Flow and the Making of Meaning*, 1.

1

Executive Team Execution

"The winning strategy combines analytically sound, ambitious, but logical goals with methods that help people experience new, often very ambitious goals, as exciting, meaningful, and uplifting—creating a deeply felt determination to move, make it happen, and win, now."[1]

—John Kotter

Like most productivity models and frameworks, our model of leadership excellence is based on the assumption that results increase when we improve capabilities, define excellence, and measure success. This may sound simple, but some approaches lack a strong measurement component because leadership can be hard to quantify. As we mentioned in the Introduction, our model includes two main parts that address the needs for functional/unit leadership and leadership team excellence. Figure 1.1 further illustrates that each side has three parts: Definitions of Success, the Implementation System, and Measurements of Success.

Our overall model of leadership excellence covers both team and functional leadership. For the rest of this book, however, we focus on only the left side of the model, Leadership Team Excellence, as pictured in Figure 1.2.

Leadership Excellence

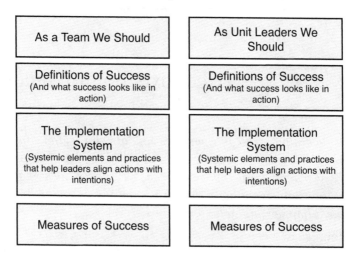

Figure 1.1   Key elements of leadership excellence as applied to individual and team performance

Leadership Team Excellence

Figure 1.2   Key elements of leadership team excellence, which together create an engine for execution

Each component of the model is important. When used as a foundation for how your leadership team operates, the model drives execution. Here is a brief description of the three sections of the model:

1. **Definitions of Success**—Included in the Definitions of Success are 1) descriptions of what great leadership is and the overall impact leaders ought to have and 2) detailed behavioral examples of what excellence looks like in action. The second part of the definition is often missing and can be used to calibrate meaning and understanding. This description of success should be illustrative but not prescriptive. For example, you might set the expectation that meeting conversations ought to be lively, focused, and help move the work forward. This description tells us something about the desired quality of the conversation but not the specific techniques we should use to create this outcome.

2. **The Implementation System**—The Implementation System section of the model seems to be the most misunderstood and least used component. Ironically, it is also where you can generate the fastest results. The Implementation System is a term we use for the many systemic tools leaders use to create results from strategies, such as roles, measures, processes, culture, rewards, communication methods, analysis, planning, internal and external benchmarking, and resources allocation. Figure 1.3 shows a sampling of the types of systems that make up your implementation system.

    Each one of these systems in the bottom portion of the chart in Figure 1.3 can and should be aligned to reinforce the desired culture and manifest your strategic initiatives.

3. **Measures of Success**—Measures of success are a part of the implementation system but worthy of their own section in our model. As you will discover later in the chapter, there are many ways leadership teams can measure their success and a few important measures that we recommend you add to your leadership team dashboard.

Your Systemic Implementation System

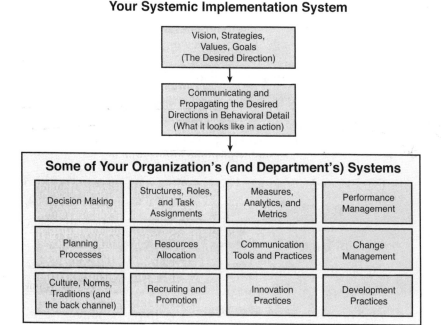

Figure 1.3   Elements of an organization's implementation system

In this first chapter, we offer examples of leadership team definitions of success and measures of success. The rest of the book is dedicated to providing many specific recommendations and examples for
your team's implementation system. For example,

- Chapter 2, "The Clash of Titans: Executive Teaming," focuses
  on methods for excellent executive teaming (systemic element
  = relationships and partnerships).

- Chapter 3, "Meetings Are Money," helps you make the most of
  your meetings together (systemic element = communication
  processes).

- Chapter 4, "Culture Is the Context and Often the Answer,"
  offers a model and recommendations for how to build the
  desired organizational culture (systemic element = culture).

- Chapter 5, "They Are All Moments of Truth," presents our
  experience and ideas regarding recognizing and seizing individual leadership opportunities (systemic elements = time allocation, decision making, and relationships).

- Chapter 6, "Getting Better Together," stresses the importance of leadership team member coaching and development and offers time-efficient strategies (systemic element = skill development).
- Chapter 7, "Creating an Agile Organization," offers a model for organizational agility and ways leadership teams can build agility (systemic elements = planning, strategies, culture, roles, change management, processes).
- Chapter 8, "Leadership Team Strategies for Remaining Union-Free," shares our deep experience about how leadership teams can best help their organizations remain union-free (systemic elements = employee relations/HR, culture, performance management, skill development, management).

Has this list given you a better idea of what we mean by the Implementation System? The more you think of the many systems and practices you use as part of your implementation system, the more likely you will be to proactively assess and tweak them to produce better results. There is a bit of magic, we find, in calling it the implementation system. When you call something a chair, even if it is a stump, people are more inclined to sit on it. By linking your practices and systemic tools together and calling it an implementation system, you are more likely to see it as an important part of your execution engine—which it is.

Definitions of Success

As we mentioned in the Introduction, we want to help you and your fellow leadership team members make big things happen with the 5% of your work time that you spend together. When we thought about the benefits we wanted this book to provide, we asked ourselves several questions. What does executive team excellence look like? How should an executive team measure how well it is leading together? How ought their definition of success cascade to middle management and lower level teams? What burden ought leadership teams own to model extraordinary teaming skills? What does being productive look like for a senior-level team? If a new middle manager observes the senior leadership team together, what conclusions would we like him or her to make? We explore the answers to these questions in this and subsequent chapters.

Let's start with how we define leadership team excellence, which is the same thing as its definition of success. A good definition of success describes desired outcomes and impact, intentions for how the team ought to accomplish goals, and indications for how outcomes relate to and reinforce each other. Examples of these elements are

- **Desired outcomes**—Financial outcomes, growth, market share, new product development and introductions, quality, safety, retention, bench strength, success of decisions, desired culture, management team capacity.
- **Desired impacts**—Role modeling excellence, setting the tone for how people ought to communicate, establishing and demonstrating the organization's moral compass, establishing a general "vibe" for the type of workplace it will be, how leadership practices either enable or hinder other people's work, demonstrating good/inadequate sense of urgency.
- **Intentions for how the team ought to accomplish goals**— Mission, values, strong relationships, a preference for strong analysis or collaboration, an intolerance for immature clashing of styles or silo mentality, preference for short- or long-term thinking in ways that develop skills and cohesiveness.
- **Indications for how outcomes relate to and reinforce each other**—Intermediary outcomes (impact and how the work ought to be done) will improve thinking, analysis, decision accuracy, team efficiencies, and responsiveness, which will have a positive impact on bottom-line business results.

While it is common for leadership teams to track financial results, few take the time to define excellence in terms of organizational or management team capacity. Paying attention to the balance sheet is critical but not enough to tell teams if they are leading in ways that set their organizations up for long-term success. For example, great teams care about

- **Strategic implementation**—The extent the organization's goals and intentions are brought to fruition and the efficiency with which they do this.

- **Growing the business**—Whether the team moves the organization forward in terms of innovation, growth, and expansion of capabilities. The extent to which nagging issues and threats are reduced and opportunities are seized and acted upon.

- **Success of decisions**—The quality of decision-making practices and decision impact over time. Do decisions serve effective planning, action, and results? Is the team adequately decisive?

- **Creating and propagating the mission, vision, and a rolling strategic plan**—It is not enough to create a strategy and a list of values; these tools of focus must become a part of decisions, action, and the culture to drive results.

- **Removing barriers**—Enabling the management team and their ability to implement strategies.

- **Defining the ideal culture**—Building and aligning organization practices to reinforce the ideal culture.

- **Communicating excellence**—Modeling the way for all professionals, especially middle management.

- **Building leadership and managerial talent**—Creating and using bench strength analysis and succession planning for key positions and personnel.

- **Building relationships and the leadership team's reputation**—Within the organization and with key stakeholders.

- **Intra-team coaching, mentoring, and collaboration**—How effectively team members help each other build skills.

- **Building organizational agility**—Within the leadership team and throughout the organization.

We know you care about these things; most leaders do. The important question is whether you and your fellow team members define your success based on them? If not, how do you determine and measure your impact? And while it might not be realistic to spend time discussing and measuring all of these indicators of success, we recommend you agree on which are most important and would best enable your organization and management team to do their best work.

You make decisions together, you create and communicate the vision, you solve urgent problems, and you set the tone for your organization. You and your fellow team members will be best served with a definition of success that encompasses all these desired outcomes. With a compelling definition of success you will be armed with a helpful filter for determining how to best spend time as a leadership team. In addition, your definition of success can become a starting point for a similar description of middle management excellence. Create and share this with your management teams to improve their clarity and focus. We recommend that you review your definition of success quarterly and share it with your Board, management teams, employees, and other key stakeholders.

"You can't build a reputation on what you're going to do."
—Henry Ford

Measures of Success

Now that we have recommended creating and sharing your team's definition of success, let's explore how to sufficiently measure leadership team achievement. By "sufficiently," we mean that your measures of success should tell you how well the team is performing as a group and whether your precious and expensive time together is well spent. Many leadership teams do not measure their effectiveness at all, which we find surprising given that you likely expect this type of measurement and proactive improvement from the teams that report to you. Why the difference? As we mentioned in the Introduction, many leadership teams don't even think of themselves as a team. If you don't identify as a team, you might not think team measures are important. We endeavor to change this! When the leadership team is highly effective, their positive impact on the organization is immense.

Sample Definition of Success

A client of ours was struggling to come together as a strong senior team and suffered from a lack of good teaming skills. The middle management team felt that clashing styles and an apparent lack of mutual respect and collaboration between senior leadership team members got in the way of them doing their best work. In addition, this organization did not have adequate bench strength for the top three levels in the organization. What follows is the definition of success we created for this client. (We have changed their name in this example.)

Leadership Team Definition of Success at Acme

Acme is poised for growth, and these are exciting times. How we lead together will determine the size, success, and reputation of Acme. This definition of success is the description of the expectations we have for one another and that we believe will best serve our goals and the organization.

One of our key responsibilities is to create and communicate a clear and compelling mission and strategic plan for the organization. From this big picture we can define the desired culture and values we feel ought to guide our work. Communication is our currency for leading. Our words and actions should consistently reinforce the vision, strategies, and values. We must clarify and frequently communicate our financial, quality, service, and product development goals with staff and other key stakeholders. Results orientation is also important for our success. When we role model focus and a sense of urgency for what's most important, our middle managers and teams will do the same for their areas of responsibility. As a senior team, we need to continuously build our skills for strategic planning and decision making by considering more points of view and reflecting on and evaluating the success of our past decisions.

We know that we cannot expect our employees to be more engaged or committed than we are (and act), so we will role model our passion for and dedication to the business with energy, engagement, and perseverance. Our employees will own their work and results. When they understand what excellence looks like and feels like, they make a difference, are able to grow, and have a strong connection to their work, manager, and coworkers. We will create an environment where employees can actively participate in making this a better business and workplace while building relationships with their peers and managers. How we work together as a leadership team sets the tone for our middle managers and employee teams. If we have and demonstrate strong and productive relationships, they will do the same. We will continuously work on our relationships and build mutual respect that brings out the best in us all. We know that our reputation within the organization is critical to our success and will build relationships with employees at all levels of the organization such that all employees know who their leaders are, what they care about, and how they intend to lead.

Our ability to respond to emerging opportunities will be determined by our nimbleness. To build an agile organization, we need to be an agile leadership team and realign our practices and priorities and have the courage and comfort to reevaluate prior decisions. We will show our managers and employees how to say "yes" to what's important by saying "no" to projects and tasks that no longer should top our list.

Our middle management team is our organization's engine, and we will take great care and energy to ensure their skills and capabilities continue to develop. As a senior leadership team, we collectively own developing key talent and ensuring we have organizational bench strength. Talent development is not just a functional leadership responsibility; it is an important measure of success for our team, and we will together spend time, energy, and resources to ensure we are building talent and growing our high potential employees.

As a senior leadership team, the time we spend together is precious and expensive. We will use our meeting time wisely and in ways that move the organization forward. We will not tolerate ineffective agendas and will not let differences of style or opinions get in the way of our collaboration and partnership. When we meet with our staff teams, we will hold others and ourselves to the same high expectations and standards.

If you read this brief definition of success before every leadership team meeting, how might that change your actions and behaviors? You will want to create your own definition of success that emphasizes the goals and success factors that are more important to your team's success. Some parts of your definition of success will change as your team and organization grows and changes.

[handwritten margin note: Starting Books]

The opposite is also true. An underperforming leadership team causes big problems and can wreck the organization's performance and culture.

It is easy to over or under-do metrics. We are wary of creating excess measures and know that leadership teams don't have time for elaborate systems and processes. Later in the chapter we recommend a focused list of measures for you to consider. To get a better feel for the type of variability that exists with how teams measure their success, we surveyed members of several dozen leadership teams about how they measure their success. They were asked which of the following performance measures they currently use to define their success *as a team*:

- ☐ Financial performance
- ☐ Safety
- ☐ Quality
- ☐ Customer service
- ☐ The team's reputation with customers or stakeholders
- ☐ Employee satisfaction
- ☐ The team's reputation within the organization
- ☐ Completion of major initiatives
- ☐ Strength of team relationships

- ☐ Team cohesion
- ☐ Strategic implementation
- ☐ Success of decisions made
- ☐ Retention

We found that the leaders vastly over-reported measures they use to measure leadership team success. In other words, they said they measured indicators of team success that they don't actually measure. In follow-up conversations, we learned two things: First, that when they thought something was important, like strategic implementation, they said they measured it. (We think that they think they do measure it!) Second, we learned that if someone else in the organization measured these indicators, they said they used the results to determine their team's success. For example, if the HR department tracks retention, then it is also a measure of team success. But if the measure is never discussed in the context of what the leadership team has or has not done to impact these performance indicators, then it is not a measure of team success. When pressed, most survey participants agreed that they did not measure leadership team success at all.

This is an important and potentially powerful distinction. If you never talk about how the team is doing and how its success ought to be measured, you will miss an opportunity to proactively improve your collective impact. If your team is like those we surveyed, you might want to start slow with adding measures. If you do not currently measure leadership team success, begin talking about it and select a small number of measures on which to initially focus.

While we were not surprised by the inaccuracy of these survey responses, the information gave us lots to talk about when working with leaders. The idea that leadership teams ought to measure team-related performance beyond financial metrics is not common, and some leaders seem at first reluctant—but then talk themselves into it

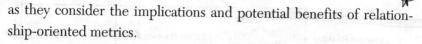

as they consider the implications and potential benefits of relationship-oriented metrics.

To continue to dig deeper, we put together a focus group of leaders and leadership development professionals and asked them one question: "How should leadership teams measure their success?" They brainstormed their answers and then discussed a list of metrics that included business results, leadership impact, and teaming outcomes. They were most passionate and vocal about how important it is for leadership teams to model the way—to set and represent the ideal tone and culture. Our focus group saw leadership teams as having the burden and opportunity to be the compass for their organizations in terms of focus and results and also how the work is conducted and the company culture found in each organization. They also felt that peer leaders ought to be more accountable to each other in terms of their interdependencies. We agree!

Many of the focus group's ideas are represented in this forthcoming list of success indicators. The trick, of course, is how to actually measure them. If you do not pay attention to how teaming impacts your organization, for example, you will not have the feedback you need to solve problems and improve team effectiveness. Every organization will have slightly different ways to measure success indicators. Figure 1.4 offers a list of measures segmented by four categories: business results, daily team effectiveness, talent development, and the workplace.

We recommend that leadership teams select, track, discuss these to improve at least one measure in each of the four sections as a way of improving their team success and impact. Each metric in your team scorecard should relate back to the organization's mission and strategies and should measure whether you are manifesting your definition of success. Let's review each scorecard metric further.

Create leadership team scorecard

Business Results	Daily Team Effectiveness	Talent Development	The Workplace
Financial results	Decision success	Bench strength and succession	Organizational culture
Customer retention and satisfaction	Relationship building	Management team capacity	Employee engagement and retention
Strategic implementation	Team reputation	Leadership team growth	Organizational agility

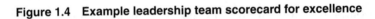

Figure 1.4   Example leadership team scorecard for excellence

Section 1: Business Results

As a category, business results focuses on outcomes that are at the core of your strategic plan. This category will likely feel most natural to measure as a team. We have offered several suggestions for how leadership teams should use these measures to gauge their collective success. The three parameters we explore in this category include financial performance, customer retention and satisfaction, and strategic implementation.

Financial Performance

We are not going to spend a lot of time and space talking about how you should measure your financial results, as this is one type of metric that nearly all leadership teams already do and on which they focus. Some focus on profit, market share, EVA, EBITDA, gross margin, and so on. A change that you might need to make is to look at these measures in terms of how they indicate the effectiveness of the leadership team. For example, let's say that you're one quarter into your fiscal year and your revenues are under goal. You know that there are several factors affecting revenues and have discussed potential ways to turn things around. The fixes will involve people from several departments including marketing, sales, and operations. The poor revenue results are also an indicator of how the leadership team is operating, right? What is it about the way the team is working, the decisions it has made, the way it is spending its time together, and where it places a sense of urgency that has contributed to current revenue results? While you might not need to change your financial measures, it will serve the team and organization well if you use these measures to look into the mirror and understand how the leadership team is impacting results.

Customer Retention and Satisfaction

Many organizations conduct and generate reports from customer service surveys. The scores are charted, communicated, and might even become catalysts for future action and improvement. And although it is not uncommon for organizations to collect this data, it is less likely that the leadership team measures *their* success based on customer satisfaction scores.

There's an even more important issue to explore here, though, and that is that our current measure might not be telling us what we need to know. The world is changing, and our customers' expectation for how they want to interact and do business with us is also changing. Do you know how well you capture their attention? Do you measure customer engagement and retention? Do you have a way of knowing how many of your customers become company evangelists and why? In his book, *Delivering Happiness: A Path to Profits, Passion, and Purpose*, Zappos CEO Tony Hsieh, writes that customer service ought to be instilled into all aspects of the business. Do we measure the part the accounting department plays in manifesting the organization's vision of service? How would we approach figuring this out? Here are just two of Hsieh's 10 ways to instill customer service:

"Don't measure call times, don't force employees to upsell, and don't use scripts."

"Give great service to everyone; customers, employees, and vendors."[2]

If you agree with Hsieh's assertions, how might that change how you measure customer service? We know of a healthcare organization, for example, that measures whether employees use customer service scripts or predetermined, preferred words and phrases as an indicator of customer service. We wonder if they have ever measured whether the script language makes customers feel better served and more satisfied.

We are not suggesting that every organization follow the Zappos model for customer service, but we would encourage you to question your current measures to ensure they are giving you the information you need to determine if the service you are committed to providing is what your customers are experiencing. With helpful and relevant measures, the leadership team can discuss progress and make better decisions about changes that will enhance your results and customer retention.

Once you have the right measures, look inward again to ask how the leadership team is impacting customer service results. What are you modeling? How are your decisions impacting how customers are dealt with? Take the customer service scores personally, as indicators of what the team is or is not doing well. The healthcare organization we mentioned that values the use of their scripts is likely reinforcing the importance of compliance to scripts starting at the top. If this measure ends up not actually improving customer satisfaction, the leadership team is inadvertently having a negative impact on results.

 ### Strategic Implementation

This measure focuses on the strategic plan and, more specifically, whether the leadership team brings their intentions to fruition. Many teams do a pretty good job of tracking major initiatives, as there is often a lot of focus on them. In addition, we recommend that leaders look at the overall strategic plan and ask, "How are we doing as a team?" Specifically, the leadership team should ask

- Overall, how is the strategic plan coming along? Where are we? Are we on track, and which areas need more of our time and focus?

- Is the strategic plan still relevant, and are we doing a good job keeping it up to date?

- As a team, have we ensured that our middle managers and other employees understand the strategic plan and the parts they play in its implementation?

- As a team, how well are we modeling an appropriate sense of urgency for top priorities?

If you and your team run through these questions quarterly, you will find that you are more in tune to how you can best impact successful strategic implementation. In our experience, the areas that need the most attention are in keeping the plan up to date and communicating the plan and the parts others need to play. A major reason a leadership team exists is to create and implement the strategic plan. It makes sense, then, to measure the team's effectiveness against the plan's implementation and success.

Section 2: Daily Team Effectiveness

This category seeks to measure what you do with your time as a team and how well you get your team's work done. This is an area of pain for many leadership team members we have talked with but is almost never a part of team measurements. The three parameters to measure in this category include decision-making success, relationship building, and the team's reputation.

Decision-making Success

One of the most important things a leadership team does is make decisions, and yet we found few teams who measured their decision-making success. This seems like disconnect with some understandable complexities. It is a disconnect because of the importance and impact of their decisions. The complex part is figuring out what it really means to make a good decision. We spoke with Luda Kopeikina, author of *Right Decision Every Time: How to Reach Perfect Clarity on Tough Decisions*, several years ago and asked her how she defined a good decision. According to Kopeikina, a correct decision occurs when the decision maker is totally congruent with the decision. She does not measure whether a decision is correct by the outcome because we can't control the consequences; we can only control how well we looked at the problem or opportunity. She found that mature leaders, those who made more successful decisions, wholeheartedly agreed with her definition. Less experienced leaders tended to define decisions by their outcomes. How do you define decision success?

Another finding from Kopeikina's research is that more successful decision makers spend more time reflecting (or doing post mortems) on decisions. They evaluate their decisions and learn from them and believe that learning from the past is the best way to pursue mastery. Do you and your team talk about your decisions after they are made? Some might balk at the idea, calling it rehashing the past and unhelpful. We think that the key to productive reflection lies in the quality of the questions you ask. Here are several questions we recommend you and your peers consider exploring after decision making:

- Are we congruent with the decision? Why/why not?
- Did we involve the right people?
- Did we collect the right or enough information?

- Knowing what we now know, would we do things differently? If yes, how could we have discovered this information earlier?
- Did we communicate the decision fully and well?
- Did discussions leading up to the decision demonstrate good partnership and co-ownership?
- How do we feel about the outcome?

This evaluation is one way to measure the effectiveness of your decisions. Give these questions a try at a future leadership team meeting. Keep notes from each conversation and notice the trends in your answers.

Relationship Building

Relationship building might seem like a strange thing to measure because it is not often thought of as an outcome. Even so, we highly recommend that leadership teams consider this as an important indicator of their success. We go into detail on the benefits and consequences of relationship building in Chapters 2, 5, and 8. Relationships affect thinking and commitment, which in turn affect actions, which determine results. The relationships that a senior leadership team builds become a foundation and model for how well the rest of the organization will work together. In addition, your visibility and the way in which your employees come to know you (your brand—see upcoming section on reputation) is your currency for building trust, commitment, and understanding.

What should leadership teams measure to determine how well they are building relationships? While there are many useful aspects of relationship building you could measure, we recommend starting with one or more of the three choices explained here.

Quality of Relationship Building with Middle Management Team and Individuals

How much time does the leadership team (as a team and as individuals representing the team) spend with middle managers? Relationship building occurs when conversations move beyond the assigning of tasks and reporting on the project milestones. How much time are you spending getting to know each other? How much time are you spending talking about development and offering coaching and mentoring? How much time are you spending sharing ideas and collaborating together? The quality of the relationship building is determined by the variety and depth of your conversations with middle managers and how open you are with them. As the engine of your organization and key partners in improving strategic implementation, your relationships with middle managers are crucial.

Quality of Relationship Building Within the Leadership Team

How well has your team come together? How well do you know and understand each other's hot buttons, idiosyncrasies, and unique strengths? Mutual respect improves with relationship building because it gives us a richer context from which to make sense of each other's actions. Do you know what's driving your peers? Do they know what's driving you and what you most worry about? While the team does not need to become best friends, spending some informal time together will improve team performance.

Quality of Visibility and Informal Communications with All Levels of the Organization

Do frontline employees know the members of the leadership team? Do operation employees know the marketing and finance leaders? Is the work of the team known and understood by all employees? Do employees feel like they know the senior leaders as human beings? (Do they know something about you?)

Leadership is a social act, and it occurs through conversations. Relationships are your currency for getting the work done through people. Unfortunately, many leadership teams don't monitor and measure how well they are building their relationship reserves. As Keith Ferrazzi wrote in *Never Eat Alone: And Other Secrets to Success, One Relationship at a Time*, "You need to build it before you need it."[3] What Ferrazzi means is that relationship building is an investment in your future effectiveness as a leader. If you do not invest now, you will not be able to instantly call forth a bond with employees. We see this dynamic play out time and again during union organizing attempts. If the leadership team has not built the relationships it needs to create a connection with employees, they will lack credibility and trust when they ask employees to vote "no" to having a union represent them.

The Team's Reputation Within the Organization

As a team, your reputation is also your leadership brand, and we think it is helpful to think of your reputation in this way. As a group, you and your peers create, improve, and erode your brand. Like other product and service brands (leadership could be considered either or both), your reputation is based on past actions; current products and results; and the strength, clarity, and attractiveness of your future vision. The future is quite important, actually. Consider Richard Branson's brand for Virgin Galactic, the rocket-ship airlines that will one day bring passengers into outer space. They have not yet delivered on the promise, but their brand is quite strong and healthy. Their brand is built based on the previous actions and reputations of the founders and key leaders, on current communications and product development progress (check out their website at www.virgingalactic. com), and on a highly compelling vision for space travel for the (wealthy) masses.

To measure your leadership team reputation, think about how you might measure the strength and health of any brand. The following shows several typical measures of brand strength and how we translate these to measure the reputation of the leadership team.

- **Does it increase revenue?**—Is the leadership team increasing corporate results and value? Are they modeling excellence such that middle managers and employees follow their lead? Are they building the skill base of talent?

- **Does it increase the amount of business you are getting?**—Is the leadership team driving growth of the business? Are they using their time in ways that improve progress?

- **Does it strengthen customer loyalty and reduce new customer acquisition costs through word-of-mouth referrals?**—Does the leadership team improve customer loyalty? Does it improve retention of top talent and make the company a more sought after employer?

- **Does it represent a competitive edge?**—Is the strength of the leadership team a competitive edge?

- **Does it attract new customers?**—Are investors, potential partners, and prospective employees attracted to the organization because of the leadership team?

- **Does it offer a clear value proposition?**—Inside of the organization, is the leadership team seen as a well-performing and effective group? As one of the largest expenses in the company, are they regarded as being a great team? Do people want to follow the leadership team?

- **Can it break through the noise of competing brands?**—Given all the various ways employees receive direction, inspiration, and role modeling, does the leadership team's efforts represent major positive influences for middle managers and employees? Have there been negative or anti-brand experiences that get in the way of the leadership team's brand?

Do you see how the brand metaphor works for evaluating your leadership team's reputation? We like this approach because it nudges you to think about a variety of factors that affect how people feel about the leadership team. Your employees care about many things including how well you are leading the organization (broad) and whether you come across as caring and a good human being at the annual picnic (narrow). As a starting point, select two or three brand element questions that you want to focus on, observe, measure, and improve.

Whose Eyes?

An important question we recommend every leadership team asks is, "What do we look like through the eyes of our employees?" This, too, is a good way to measure reputation. If you use 360-degree assessments or an employee engagement survey, you might find very helpful feedback about how your employees perceive your team leadership. If you do not use these tools or they don't contain relevant questions, you should find another way of getting their feedback. And here is one caveat to the usefulness of the 360-degree feedback: You will only learn what the next level of management thinks about you, not how your frontline employees see you. But you need that feedback, too. At the time we are writing this chapter, we are working with a client who was recently blindsided by the realization that their employees neither know nor trust them. We think, after talking with their staff, that this is a simple case of ignoring the masses—they focused on building relationships with just their middle managers. Chapter 5, offers ideas for how to build strong relationships—and your team's reputation—with employees at all levels.

Section 3: Talent Development

This category is perhaps the narrowest, focusing on how well the leadership team builds talent. Many organizations say they are committed to developing their people, and fewer leadership teams act and lead accordingly, even when they intend to support development. The three measures we explore in this category include bench strength and succession planning, management team capacity, and leadership team growth.

Bench Strength and Succession Planning

Building talent is a core leadership team responsibility but is often delegated to the human resources department, who should own certain aspects of development. When middle managers see that their leaders don't focus on building talent, they often follow suit, and employee capabilities begin to lag and languish. You cannot continue to be a competitive organization if your staff does not increase its skills. And there is another benefit of good talent development practices—growing and learning is an important intrinsic motivator for employees, especially Generations X and Y. Some leaders are quite clear about their roles in developing talent (GE's former CEO, Jack Welch famously said that building talent was his main job), while others seem content to leave development to HR. What do you and your peers think? What impression would your managers get about talent management from observing the leadership team?

"Actions" is a key word because to measure your team's ability to build talent, you need to assess your systemic actions along with how you reinforce and support developmental experiences. This is especially true for succession planning processes, which are development tools for preparing key talent for future roles. Many more leadership teams create succession charts than actively manage succession. Creating the chart is step one of 100 steps. Bench strength is an expression of how strong or vulnerable your skill base is. The following offers a sample succession planning and bench strength scorecard for you to consider.

Talent Management Outcome: You use a system for evaluating talent (as distinct from performance) on at least a yearly basis. The leadership team is actively engaged in this process and dedicates time throughout the year for talent reviews.

Measurement Criteria: Defined process in place and being used. The output of the review offers information needed to create useful development plans. The middle management team believes that this process is important to the leadership team and believes they place a high priority the talent review.

Current Measure:

_____

_____

Talent Management Outcome: You actively partner with HR to create and regularly update the key skills and competencies that are critical for success for leaders and managers.

Measurement Criteria: There are relevant and useful position/level skills profiles that incumbents and high potentials can use to guide and own their development plans.

Current Measure:

_____

_____

Talent Management Outcome: Key talent, individuals who are sometimes called high potentials or potential successors, is identified as part of the talent review. The leadership team oversees their progress and development and collectively discusses and agrees on how to best develop high potentials as well as cooperates with each other to enable developmental experiences to occur.

Measurement Criteria: The leadership team knows and agrees on who their key players are. Their progress is discussed by the leadership team several times per year. Positions and developmental experiences are created if needed to prepare key players. When key positions open up, there is an internal candidate ready to fill the position.

Current Measure:

_____

_____

Talent Management Outcome:

Talent gaps are identified as part of the talent review (including emerging skill needs). The leadership team creates and implements a plan to fill the talent gap.

Measurement Criteria: The leadership team has a good feel for the skills they need to grow or acquire. Skills gaps are closed.

Current Measure:

_____

_____

_____

Some organizations do much more than these basic succession planning steps, and many do far less. Does your leadership team play an active role in identifying and developing your top talent? One of our clients has their top-level leaders meet quarterly for half a day to discuss high potentials and successor readiness. This is a big-time commitment but also a huge value. This organization has very strong bench strength and can often make promotion announcements within a week after a position is identified as becoming vacant.

"The 'business' of leaders at all levels is to help those in their charge develop beyond their dreams—which in turn almost automatically leads to 'all that other stuff,' such as happy customers, happy stockholders, happy communities."[4]

—Tom Peters

Management Team Capacity

You and your fellow leadership team members can and should have a big impact on the development and growth of the management team. While individual managers should own their development and the training department should own providing quality relevant development experiences, the leadership team's responsibilities are more strategic and broad. As mentioned previously in this chapter, the management team is your engine for strategic implementation, and some number of managers need to be ready to become the leaders of tomorrow. What's the role of the leadership team in making sure that the skills of the management team are adequate to accomplish goals today and tomorrow? We believe that leadership teams ought to partially measure their success based on whether they have

- Created an environment where development is valued and supported. Is the training department the only one pushing for training? We would rather see that the leadership team and then individual managers are banging down the doors of the training department to ensure managers are trained well.

- Discussed and actively participate in talent reviews of the management team (see previous measure).
- Taken on the roles of mentors and coaches for at least one manager per leadership team member (and others are paired up with peer managers) and that these roles are known and discussed as part of the development strategy.
- Identified management development as a strategic initiative and have identified critical skills needs or gaps and key initiatives to address the need.

Is your management team able to implement the strategic plan? Do they have the skills to build a strong employee relations environment that will enable you to remain union-free? How well do your managers drive and manage change? Are they building or reducing your organization's nimbleness? You want to know the answers to these questions. In fact, the answers to these questions disclose quite a lot about the effectiveness of a leadership team. Once you understand their current skills and training needs, you can determine what the leadership team ought to do to improve your management team's capacity.

Leadership Team Growth

The higher you go in the organization, the less feedback and training you tend to receive. The need to develop does not diminish, but the organizational systems and resources for development tend to be aimed at middle- and frontline-level employees. This dynamic is normal and appropriate but also means that the people who most need to stay on top of their game are basically on their own to determine how they should grow. Individual leaders should own their development, but peers on the leadership team can play an important role in providing coaching and helping them stay accountable to their development. Leadership team members ought to help each other become better leaders and collectively engage in development activities.

How well does your leadership team ensure that members grow ever year? Do you have a measurement in place to ensure that your development does not get pushed aside by other priorities? We cover this topic in great detail in Chapter 6, but start to ask yourself what one or two ways you could track whether and how well the leadership team improves the skills and abilities of its members. Should senior executives have development plans? Why not? It might look different (hint, see Chapter 6) than the development plans used at lower levels in the organization, but a simple plan could help you and your peers stay focused and in action. Are there one or two development activities that the entire team would benefit from each year? Absolutely, and we recommend you commit to doing this.

At the end of each year, you should ask yourselves, "What have we done to help each other become stronger and more effective leaders?" You want to be able to list several specific actions and ways you helped each other focus on growth. A side benefit of measuring leadership team growth is that you should become more self-aware and open. This will serve you in many ways and help make your relationships stronger because we act differently (better) when we are more self-aware.

Section 4: The Workplace

This category focuses on context—on the environment that leaders shape and build. Many of the leaders we spoke to agreed that setting the right tone and building a strong culture are key leadership responsibilities. So it is time you measured your team success based on these goals as well! The three measures we explore in this category include organizational culture, employee engagement and retention, and organizational agility.

Organizational Culture

Chapter 4 focuses on how leadership teams create culture. As a team, you can and should measure how well you are creating the desired culture. Because culture is so important and also difficult to change, you might need to invest more time and energy into measuring your team performance for this indicator. Here are two ways you can measure your impact on creating the desired culture:

1. *Define and communicate the desired culture*—Make sure that the desired culture is reinforced throughout the organization. To measure this activity, ask employees at all levels to describe the current and desired culture. How well does this match your intentions?

2. *Model the desired culture*—Do you lead consistent with the culture you seek? Does the leadership team make decisions congruent with the desired culture? To measure your success, ask middle managers and frontline employees to describe what they think is most important to leaders based on their actions and decisions.

You might be thinking that you can get some of this information from your employee engagement survey, and perhaps you can. We doubt, however, that most traditional engagement survey questions will give you a clear idea about how well the leadership team is building the ideal culture. Instead, we would recommend that you ask your OD (organization development) or training department to conduct focus group sessions every year to collect the data. These are tough questions for people to respond to in writing, but they are the right ones to ask.

Employee Engagement and Retention

Should a leadership team measure their success based on retention data? Yes! Absolutely! You and your peers make a big impact on why and whether people join or leave the organization. Studies have consistently shown that employees *join companies* and *leave managers* and that a "bad manager" is the most common reason employees start looking for another job.

You might be asking how that explains why the leadership team should measure their success based on employee engagement and retention. When bad managers are allowed to be bad managers for months or even years, this is a failing of the leadership team—and can only happen when one of the following conditions exists:

- Standards for managerial excellence are not known or communicated.
- How managers are evaluated does not hold them accountable for standards of excellence.
- Talent reviews do not deal with problem performers.
- The standards of excellence are not adequate.
- Relationships between leaders and managers is inadequate.

The leadership team owns all of these outcomes. A bad manager cannot exist (for long) when standards for managerial excellence are clear, managers are held accountable, talent reviews deal with problem performers, and the standards for management are high and compelling.

In addition, employee engagement and retention is impacted by how intrinsically motivating the workplace is, and this is driven by decisions and actions that come from the leadership team. There are many ways that the leadership team impacts employee engagement. Leigh Branham and Mark Hirschfeld, authors of *Re-Engage: How America's Best Places to Work Inspire Extra Effort in Extraordinary Times*, found that senior leaders may, in fact, have a more significant impact on employee engagement than the middle managers and supervisors that are their direct managers.

> In our experience, however, it is the senior leadership team that creates the culture, sets the tone, inspires trust and confidence, or undermines it. We believe that senior leaders—CEOs and their direct reports—most strongly influence the very managers they hold accountable for engaging employees. If engaging employees were a card game, the senior leaders would be dealing the face cards.[5]

Branham and Hirschfeld also quoted research that cognitive engagement, which occurs when employees feel good about the direction and strategies of the organization, is as powerful and important as emotional engagement.

Many organizations track retention and reasons for turnover (via exit interviews, for example) and use employee engagement surveys to measure engagement. If your organization has these tools available, you might be able to use them to assess whether and how well the leadership team is doing to keep top talent happy and productive. Many engagement surveys, however, assess the impact managers have on engagement but fail to ask the questions the leadership team could use to measure its performance. If you can, add relevant questions to your current tools to avoid over surveying your employees. We have found focus groups very helpful in assessing how well the leadership team improves employee engagement and retention.

Organizational Agility

We share a model of organizational agility as well as ways you can improve it in Chapter 7. Building a nimble workplace requires that you make many systemic changes so that your practices are frequently updated and re-evaluated. Agility is not a mindset; it is a practice. To measure the leadership team's impact on agility, then, you need to determine your role in building agile practices. There is an assessment in Chapter 7 that you can use as a benchmark measure of how agile the organization is. Then determine, as a team, which actions you should focus on that might help improve agility. Re-evaluate agility at the end of the year and measure any progress.

It would also be helpful to assess how nimble you are as a team. How flexible are you, and does the organization see you as an enabler or as a team that slows progress? We did focus group discussions for a client a few years ago and did several sessions with employees at all levels except senior leadership. We consistently heard that the leadership team was stale and a barrier to getting things done. They were regarded as the least agile part of the organization! When talking to the leadership team, they did not see themselves in this way. In fact, they felt as though the team might be using this complaint as an excuse for inaction. Wow, how could two so different views exist? As a leadership team, you want to make sure you are not hindering your organization's agility, and you want to identify and fix any perception differences. How will you do this unless you measure your impact on agility?

Which Indicators Should You Measure?

We have just reviewed 12 types of measurement across four categories of performance you and your team should consider: business results, daily team effectiveness, talent development, and the workplace. But don't measure all 12; select one or two for each performance category as a starting point. If you don't currently talk about leadership team effectiveness, start with just one measure per category and spend more time discussing each category and measure. The idea of evaluating the team's impact might take some getting used to, so give you and your fellow team members the space to learn the best ways to hold each other accountable.

To kick things off, hand out this chapter as prereading before your next leadership team meeting and spend 45 minutes discussing it. Create your own leadership team scorecard and make reviewing it a regular part of your team dialogue. Unlike your monthly financial reports, many of these measures will need to be discussed every three or six months.

"Above all else, a leader is the chief energy officer. Energy, after all, is contagious—especially so if you're a leader, by virtue of your disproportionate position and power. The way you're feeling at any given moment profoundly influences how the people who work for you feel."[6]

—Tony Schwartz

Endnotes

1. John Kotter, *A Sense of Urgency*, 47.

2. Tony Hsieh, *Delivering Happiness: A Path to Profits, Passion, and Purpose*, 147.

3. Keith Ferrazzi, *Never Eat Alone: And Other Secrets to Success, One Relationship at a Time*, 42.

4. Tom Peters, *The Little Big Things: 163 Ways to Pursue Excellence*, 143.

5. Leigh Branham and Mark Hirschfeld, *Re-Engage: How America's Best Places to Work Inspire Extra Effort in Extraordinary Times*, 67.

6. Tony Schwartz, "The CEO Is the Chief Energy Officer." *A Better Way of Working* blog, entry posted June 2, 2010, www.theenergyproject.com/blog/ceo-chief-energy-officer.

2

The Clash of Titans: Executive Teaming

 "When two elephants fight it is the grass that suffers."
—African Proverb

We talk to professionals in hundreds of organizations every year, and we have noticed an interesting pattern. When mentioning the topic of executive teaming, we tend to get applause from middle managers and frontline professionals but a less enthusiastic interest level from leaders. Teaming, perhaps, is like flossing your teeth—critical but not on the top of the list of things to do. Also many leadership teams either don't know they have teaming issues or know but aren't committed to correcting them. When a senior-level team behaves in a dysfunctional way, it affects the entire organization and processes like decision making, work hand-offs, and interdepartmental collaboration. Even so, the notion of executive teaming skills is somewhat uncommon because most executives are promoted and measured based on individual efforts and success.

What Is Executive Teaming?

Teaming affects how well a group thinks together. How well a group thinks together affects their decisions and outcomes. Team skills, therefore, enable results. We use the term *teaming* to represent the beliefs, behaviors, practices, and habits that impact how well a group of professionals work together in a group. Communication practices are a part of teaming. Relationships affect teaming. The way we respond to those with similar or dissimilar tendencies impacts the team. How we go about getting the team's work done is an aspect of teaming.

Executive teaming, then, is a set of beliefs, practices, and skills that help leadership team members work better together. You might think that once someone has risen to a high level in the organization that he or she should already have learned excellent teaming skills, but this is often not the case. In fact, talented executives are often praised more for their individual accomplishments. Some organizations have a high tolerance for poor teamwork at the top levels. This is hard to understand given that executives who do not play well in the ivory sand box cause a lot of problems.

Dysfunction Reverberates

When a team does not work well together, many people are impacted. The team does not do its best work. Conversations are less fruitful, and tensions cause people to seek the meeting room exit sign instead of digging deep into important operational challenges. Upstream and downstream internal customers are affected by the dysfunction because it spills into their communications and affects the quality of the work coming from the team. Those around the team feel the pain from the team's dysfunction as the stress and tension bring down the surrounding vibe of the place. The team's failed teaming brings down even those with no direct involvement with the group. Like a pebble hitting the water, dysfunction reverberates.

Now imagine that the team members are senior leaders. The reverberation of their dysfunction is much wider and tends to "go viral" very quickly. The pebble is now a boulder with each ripple moving farther into the organization. Middle managers are affected and they may take out frustrations on their people. In Chapter 1, "Executive Team Execution," we wrote that leaders couldn't expect their managers and employees to be any more committed and passionate about the business than they demonstrate through their actions. The same adage goes for teaming. You cannot expect the rest of the organization to work well together if the leadership team itself does not seem to care enough to work well together.

Q: Do we care about working well together, why? why not

"I have learned that authenticity counts, and that the best route to an authentic life is through your scars. As you earn them, you learn to drop the B.S. in your life and to attach yourself to the substance in your life—and to the substance in those around you."[1]

—John Hope Bryant

KEY = attach myself to the substance in my life and to substance those around

---

Holding Yourself to a High Standard

Executive team dysfunction is an indicator that leaders do not care whether people work well together. This might not be an accurate interpretation of your beliefs, but how else could it be interpreted? Leadership team members are some of the most privileged employees within the company. They get paid the most, have more perks, and have been entrusted with the amazing responsibility to lead the organization—and people follow them. Yes, their jobs are very hard and may involve more pressure and risk than we care to take on, but they are privileged. If highly paid leaders do not think it is worth their time and effort to improve how well they work within their peer teams, why should anyone else?

Executive team dysfunction is irresponsible and immature. This may seem like a strong statement, and it is because we don't understand how any executive can rationalize in his or her mind how being a poor team player is acceptable. Is it OK to waste your and your peers' time because you don't like someone's style? No! Grow up, we say, when we are facilitating executive retreats and come across this type of behavior. We would like leadership team members to hold themselves to a higher standard and then have similarly high standards for the teams that report to them. It is well worth the time you need to invest to develop good teaming skills and well worth biting your tongue on occasion or putting your ego temporarily aside. It is important that leaders harmonize, not homogenize, to produce the best thinking, decisions, and outcomes. Be great together!

"Winning too much is easily the most common behavioral problem that I observe in successful people. There's a fine line between being competitive and overcompetitive, between winning when it counts and when no one's counting—and successful people cross that line with alarming frequency."[2]
—Marshall Goldsmith

Two Executive Teaming Skills

Great leadership teamwork enables leaders to reinforce desired behaviors and messages and get things done together more efficiently. Leaders are busy, so it is important to balance time spent together in collaboration and co-leadership with time when each leader focuses on his or her individual responsibilities. In this chapter we focus on a short list of teaming skills that every leadership team ought to develop and practice:

- Ensure differences don't lead to clashes.
- Practice partnership at all times.

These practices will help you and your peers build strong relationships and combat the most common causes for team dysfunction. In particular, the problem of clashing leadership styles ranks as the top issue for the teams who participated in our survey. Let's explore these two executive teaming skills in more detail.

It's All About Control

We have observed and believe that control is the source of many teaming issues. Leaders achieve their positions because they are comfortable taking charge, and many struggle to let go of control. Imagine seven executives in a room, all vying for control. As an example, we know a leader who is a poor leadership team member. We will call him Darren. Brilliant in many aspects of his job, Darren is quite immature and ineffective when it comes to teaming. Darren says he wants employees to own their projects and says they are empowered to do the work. He then micromanages these people and projects. His staff avoids telling him too much because they don't want him mucking about in their work. With peers, he practices a passive-aggressive style to seek control. He asks obviously leading questions and plays ignorant when called on the carpet by those who can see through his question to see what he really wants to say or advocate. He is known for being hard to work with and someone who will criticize most everything. He likes to get the last word in a conversation.

Darren's need to control is a problem and is affecting both his ability to lead and the reputation of his entire team. He does not get enough helpful feedback from others because they don't want to deal with him. His teaming style is a poor reflection on the leadership team because employees wonder why the CEO and his peers put up with Darren—which is a valid question. Why do they? If leadership is a social act (it is) and relationships are our currency for leading (they are), then how can someone who cannot build genuine and strong relationships be allowed to lead?

Not every control freak acts like Darren. The need to control comes across in many ways including cutting people off, over-participation during meetings, being dismissive of others, being passive-aggressive under pressure, and defensiveness. These are all unwelcome, unattractive, and irritating behaviors. If you are a control freak, think about how your tendencies might be affecting the team.

When you bring together a team of highly talented executives, who is leading and in control should change with the situation. Great leadership team members are leaders and followers, and every team needs both to perform well together.

Ensure Differences Don't Lead to Clashes

Clashing leadership styles is the most common reason for executive team dysfunction. On our leadership team survey, even the highest scoring teams reported that clashing styles got in the way of their team effectiveness. Clashes in style are differences in approach that are allowed to cause a problem for one or more team members. Not every difference in style leads to a clash. Figure 2.1 shows four ways how team member styles impact their effectiveness.

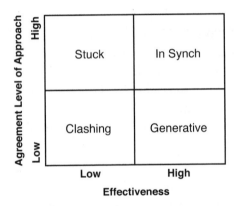

Figure 2.1   How agreement of leadership approaches and effectiveness affect the results of leadership team dialogue, decisions, and relationships

This simple model illustrates how having similar approaches can help or hinder team performance and how different approaches can also be beneficial or not. Here is an explanation of the four boxes found in the model:

- **Low Agreement/Low Effectiveness = Clashing**—Styles clash when they are different and unproductive. You know that a situation is ineffective when the differences cause team members to be dismissive, avoidant, argumentative, impatient, overly controlling, or disconnected from the conversation.

- **High Agreement/Low Effectiveness = Stuck**—Having similar approaches is not always a good thing. When styles are the same or similar but productivity is low, the leadership team will seem stuck. Their agreement is hindering their ability to push beyond their current ineffective practices and beliefs.

- **Low Agreement/High Effectiveness = Generative—** Teams can and should use differences in approach to improve creativity, decision making, and team dialogue. Differences in approach do not need to get in the way of team progress. They can, in fact, heighten it.

- **High Agreement/High Effectiveness = In Synch—** Leaders who think alike can use their stylistic shorthand to get things done well and quickly. It is important, however, to recognize when being in synch leads to blind spots or missed opportunities (when you agree too quickly and do not consider other options, information, or approaches).

Think back to your last leadership team meeting. Which of these group dynamics did you see? Which is most common? We work with a large organization that has a very stable and long-tenured leadership team. They would self-assess that their team spends a lot of time in synch. We recently held focus group discussions with their management team and discovered that they believe their leadership team spends more time stuck. Both agreed that they do not have problematic differences, but those who report to the leadership team think their leaders are too similar in approach and that they have become quite stale. How might your middle managers characterize the group dynamics of your leadership team?

Leadership teams with clashing styles can move in three directions. They can stay the same (not good), become stuck (not good), or become generative (good). Many never deal with their dysfunction, and the team and organization suffer. Some teams go from clashing to being stuck. This occurs when the differences in approach that caused their problems is replaced with avoidance or dismissiveness. The goal is to turn clashing styles into generative team thinking. = goal

One of the reasons many teams never make it to generative thinking is that each member is waiting for the other to change. When styles clash, who has the responsibility to change? The answer is you.

It only takes one person to de-escalate a clashing situation. If you wait for someone else to change, you will be disappointed, and your team may never move on because he or she is likely waiting for you to change. You might be thinking that if there is one person who is driving others on the team a little crazy that he or she should be the one to change. We believe that those who are bothered by a leader's approach also need to change.

Let's explore several common types of clashing leadership team situations and then discuss ways to move to generative thinking. Here are a few examples of common sources of irritation that lead to clashes in style:

- Two leaders who move at different paces.
- Leaders who can't shut up.
- Leaders who don't listen.
- Leaders who are perceived as being too touchy-feely—too many concerns about people.
- Leaders who dish out criticism but can't take it.
- Leaders who slow the group down by asking seemingly irrelevant questions.
- Leaders who keep rehashing issues and questions that the group has resolved.
- Leaders who are forgetful.
- Leaders who seem to have hidden and selfish motives.
- Leaders who seem self-absorbed.
- Leaders with wildly different behavioral tendencies as measured using tools such as MBTI (Myers Briggs Type Indicator), DiSC, and Social Styles.
- Leaders who seem to be all talk and little action.

Do any of these behaviors show up during your team meetings? Which one of these might describe your style or approach? More importantly, how do you respond to peers who act this way? If your answer is that you avoid them, cut them off, argue with them, or find them irritating or untrustworthy, then welcome to the world of clashing leadership styles. To reduce style clash, shoot for the following two outcomes:

✳ **1.** You and your fellow leadership team members do not let differences turn into dysfunction.

✳ **2.** You have team practices that help manage team member behaviors.

The first outcome involves how you think about differences, and the second helps you reduce the impact of certain unhelpful behaviors. To improve your tolerance of each other's styles, it is helpful to build self-awareness and get to know each other. Every team member brings strengths and weaknesses to the team, and it is helpful to learn what these are. You will find that your tolerance for someone's tendency to be a control freak, for example, improves when you understand how he or she defines his or her success. Self-awareness is critical at all levels of the organization but particularly at the senior leadership level because your strengths and weaknesses (and stylistic flaws) will have a bigger impact on others. Here are a few ways the leadership team can build self-awareness and get to know one another better:

- **Coaching**—Individual and group coaching provides self-awareness in the context of current and future goals.
- **Assessments**—Many organizations use behavioral tendency assessments (MBTI, DiSC) or 360-degree assessments to improve self-awareness.
- **Facilitated peer coaching and feedback**—Team members are in a great position to offer feedback and coaching to each other.
- **Team building**—Leadership teams often tack on team-building exercises to offsite planning meetings, and these activities can improve both self-awareness and team member familiarity.

- **Open discussion of clashing styles**—Teams can also deal directly with current sources of dysfunction by having open conversations about the behaviors that are hurting their team's productivity.

You have the choice to let differences in style become a problem or a source of strength. You can let the behaviors bother you, or you can be accepting of others' approaches. You can instantly switch from being annoyed to being open, and you can shift your mindset from one that thinks the behaviors are wrong, bad, or wasteful to one that sees that an individual might just have different ways of getting to the right decision/action. You can be the one to de-escalate the tension, and you can lead the way forward to building a more beneficially diverse team.

The second outcome you should focus on to reduce clashes in style is putting practices in place that help manage dysfunctional team behaviors. The most obvious technique for this purpose is using meeting room ground rules. In Chapter 3, "Meetings Are Money," we offer a list of recommended ground rules for leadership team meetings. You should select the ground rules that will help improve the effectiveness of your conversations. For example, if you struggle as a team to get through your agenda items, ground rules that improve agenda clarity, meeting planning, and meeting time management will be helpful. If you find that a few team members consistently dominate the conversation, you might want to adopt ground rules that help you even-out participation. If team members tend to get defensive, you can adopt ground rules that help you deliver and receive feedback and criticism in ways that reduce defensiveness.

We worked with one leadership team that had not yet learned how to be respectfully honest with one another. They lacked mutual respect, and this was obvious to us when we observed one of their team meetings (and they said they were on their best behavior that day). They had over-participators and under-participators, and in both cases the need to control seemed to be at the heart of their behaviors. They acknowledged that their meetings were not productive although they did not initially co-own that they were part of the problem and therefore needed to be part of the solution (this is common). Led by a persistent CEO who was sick of seeing his talented team underperform, the team used a combination of ground rules to manage participation, set higher goals for meeting outcomes (see Chapter 3 for more on this strategy), and build relationships to reduce the impact of their differences in approach.

Do you have clashing styles on your team? If so, we hope that you will take away from this exploration of clashing leadership styles that there are two things that need to change: your mindset and your practices. Think about the impact your team could have if clashing styles were not an issue and your team's differences actually strengthened it.

Practice Partnership at All Times

Jeff was a successful and influential vice-president of Human Resources. His fellow leadership team members valued his input and participation. They involved Jeff and his department managers in the day-to-day operations of their respective departments. Jeff's HR department was effective and well-respected to a degree rarely found in most companies. Because of the fantastic partnership between Jeff and his peers, Jeff's staff, and other departments within the organization, Jeff and his team made a positive impact on the company. However, it wasn't just a one-way street; other departments influenced Jeff and his team as well. Jeff was a powerful role model who demonstrated how peers should partner to serve one another and achieve results. Jeff also reinforced this belief in collaboration when it came time to promote and evaluate his team members. Other divisions regularly sought candidates from Jeff's department, and he frequently championed his staff for internal promotions and other positions within the company.

What made Jeff's approach even more effective was that his company had a very competitive environment. Leadership team members were generally inclined to exclude, rather than include, members of internal service teams, like HR. Had it not been for the foundation of partnership that Jeff had established, other vice-presidents in the company would not have given the HR department the same level of consideration or included them in as many initiatives.

Sue could have learned a few things from Jeff. She thought the best way to get ahead was to flatter and try to impress peers and other senior executives. She took credit for work performed by others on her team to make it appear that she was the one who had dreamed up the ideas. In meetings, she was a "yes woman," always agreeing with higher-level executives to get their nods of approval. Sue was passed over for two promotions for general management jobs for which she was technically qualified because her CEO and peers did not feel they could trust Sue or that she shared their mission for the organization. They feared that her personal drive for self-promotion would overshadow the needs of her team and those of the company. Sue had not built strong partnerships with her peers, and this hurt her and her team.

Everyone wants recognition and validation. Evening news programs love to feature stories of heroes who save the day. In the business world, however, the best and most effective way to achieve results is through teamwork—especially at the leadership level. A group of talented people rallying behind a single cause creates more success than a lone individual going off on his or her own. Leadership teams that collaborate and partner well will be more successful. Jeff understood this and was successful. Sue did not and suffered the consequences professionally.

Developing and maintaining productive partnerships is an important skill for any leader. We have said this many times throughout this book: Effective relationships are your currency for getting your work done. When peers partner, they bring out the very best in each other and get more done together. In most companies, departments are interdependent. When things go well, it is rarely because of the efforts from an individual or single department. It takes many teams, firing on all cylinders, to produce the best results. Great leadership team partnerships catalyze collaboration at all levels of the organization.

The Traits of Leadership Team Partnership

Effective partnerships help leadership teams deal with tough challenges and times of growth and opportunity. Every organization and department can benefit from the coordinated efforts of their talented leaders. Partnership goes beyond cooperation to being a purposeful act of inclusion, collaboration, and co-leadership. Merely *so true!* being helpful when solicited or asked does not make one an effective partner. Partners seek each other out and proactively involve each other in day-to-day conversations and decisions. Effective partnership emerges from a combination of several traits, which are listed as follows.

Shared Purpose

What is our shared goal?

Partners, by definition, are linked to one another. In the business world, partners need to have a sense that they are striving for the same goal. When leadership team members have a shared goal, their work together has purpose and meaning. A common target provides a foundation for partnership. Their opinions and perspectives may differ significantly, but if they are all reaching for the same goal, they can find common ground. To create a shared purpose, you and your peers need to spend time talking about and developing the strategic intentions of the organization or the piece you lead.

Shared Ownership

When two or more leaders share ownership of a result or outcome, they are more likely to work together effectively. Co-owning an

(handwritten: Q: How do we move beyond cooperation to collaboration?)

outcome takes partnership a step beyond cooperation to collaboration. Further, senior leaders who instill a sense of shared ownership between their management team members will find that this expectation helps drive greater collaboration at all levels. On the leadership team, shared ownership starts with the strategic planning process but is further enhanced when specific goals or initiatives are co-owned by two or more team members.

Mutual Trust

Leaders who trust one another will partner together more effectively. Mutual trust facilitates openness, creativity, and communication. Leadership team members do not need to agree or see things identically to develop trusting and respectful relationships with one another. Often, an appreciation of diverse thoughts and ideas improves the regard you have for one another. Leaders who collaborate well almost always share mutual trust for one another. Trust is built through the process of active and healthy collaboration and co-leadership.

(handwritten: = TRUST)

> "Yes, teamwork is important. No, teamwork doesn't mean bringing everyone with exceptional talent down to the level of the lowest common denominator."[3]
>
> —Tom Peters

Critical Thinking

(handwritten: not just "what" can you do but really are they engaging their mental skill?)

Without critical thinking, partnership is just small talk. Partners solve problems and generate new ideas together (which is why differences in style that lead to generation can be beneficial). This work occurs best when all parties are mentally stimulated, productive, and encouraged to think critically. Results are built on the mental capabilities of leadership team members working together. Engage your peers in provocative dialogue. Ask open-ended questions and seek ideas for addressing important business problems.

Shared Success and Failure

Leaders build stronger partnerships when they share the experience of winning and losing. This needs to go beyond your review of the company financial statements to include other major team accomplishments. There is nothing like seeing a strategic initiative through to completion as a team. If the project is a success, celebrating together reinforces the positive aspects of collaboration. When failures occur, you and your team should pull together to turn a loss into a learning experience and then a new set of actions. Sharing successes and failures brings the cycle of partnership full circle.

Effective Inclusion and Communication

Partners talk to each other often and take the initiative to include each other in formative planning and brainstorming conversations. As a leadership team, inclusion goes beyond going around the conference table to update each other on your respective functions. To form strong collaborative bonds, use each other as sounding boards, create plans together, and offer each other support.

The traits of partnership outlined here describe what peer collaboration looks like in action. How do you know if you have been a good partner? You can ask a trusted friend or colleague, although the answer will generally be more favorable than objective. You can also ask your manager. A better strategy is to read organizational clues. Observe how other leaders interact with one another and compare this to your experience. You can also gauge the type of partner you have been by looking at informal communication practices. How often do your peers stop by and ask for input? How open and lively are conversations with colleagues? Look for examples of successes and failures that illustrate good or poor partnership practices. By asking questions of your peers, managers, and coworkers and then watching how they respond and interact, you can begin to glean insight into the type of partner you have been.

Partnership Techniques

True!

Great partnerships do not simply happen. There are techniques that you and your fellow leadership team members can practice to build the partnership traits we just reviewed and increase the benefits of collaboration.

Don't Try to Control Peers

If you demonstrate a persistent need to control situations, people, or conversations, it will undermine effective collaboration with your peer group. Partnering is a give-and-take process in which no one gets to play boss all the time. Listen and watch for verbal and nonverbal clues that suggest other people are feeling pressured or pushed. One of the best ways to give up control in a conversation is to ask more open-ended questions and make fewer opinionated statements. In addition, enrolling your peers and creating pull (they want to collaborate) is more effective than using push methods that make them feel like they ought to partner.

Spend Time Together

Leadership is a social act. The more time that leadership team members spend working with one another, the easier and more natural the partnering process will feel. In addition, peers that get together often feel more comfortable asking for input, help, and participation than do those who only see each other at leadership team staff meetings.

Resolve Relationship Problems

Old conflicts and arguments affect the way in which people relate to one another in the present and future. You need to take the initiative to resolve any prior relationship issues in order to pave the way for better and more productive collaboration in the future. The benefits of working through and getting past prior problems with other leadership team members will more than make up for the initial discomfort of broaching the topic with them. When you resolve past differences, you clear the way for great partnership and collaboration. If you are faced with a peer who does not seem willing to improve the relationship, you can do one of three things. First, you might try a different approach. Can you look at the situation from his or her perspective? Have you isolated the key issues or problems? It may be that what you thought was the problem is not. Second, you are the only person you can control. Even if your peer is hanging onto a grudge, make sure that you continue to act and relate in a manner that is professional and collaborative. If you take the high road, he or she might come around in time.

Represent Each Other Well

Effective communication is one of the most reliable predictors of a healthy partnership. Leaders who keep one another in the loop and represent one another well in meetings and other conversations are generally great partners. Communicating with peers should be a regular part of your day. In addition to communicating well with one another, it is important for peers to communicate well on one another's behalf. Represent your peer's interests and needs in staff meetings, brainstorming sessions, and informal conversations when they are not present. You may need to defend a peer's budget choices or represent his or her opinions and concerns. Great partners do this even when they do not agree with their peers' points of view. When representing your peers in a positive light, you communicate that respect and care for colleagues is a key organizational value.

Never Bad Mouth

Never badmouth peers in front of others. It never pays to talk badly about peers, and it will burn bridges that you will need later on. Speak respectfully about other leaders, even if you think ill of them. Leaders who talk about other people behind their backs end up looking bad themselves. It is immature, unprofessional, and destructive. The saying, "What goes around, comes around," applies to workplace relationships. This is not to say that disagreements with peers should be ignored. When the leadership team meets, it is healthy to push back and challenge each other in a professional way. The best way to deal with a difference of opinion or disagreement is to communicate it directly and in a productive way to the person involved.

Own Problems and Challenges

Don't pass the buck. Few situations can put a damper on a partnership faster than being hung out to dry by a peer. We know a finance leader, Catherine, who learned this the hard way. The operations VP, we will call him Harry, blamed her for problems that were rooted in his organization. When the president confronted Catherine about this, she was unfairly put on the defensive. Harry's choice to pass blame and abdicate his own involvement in the problem diminished the level of partnership that he and Catherine would have in the future. If you have a complaint about how another leader is handling a situation, speak to that leader directly before bringing it to your boss or the team.

Be Humble

Partners know that successes come from collaboration and that all players should share the credit. While it may be true that one person's idea was the catalyst for the breakthrough, the overall success was a product of the joint effort. Leaders who ensure that everyone feels a part of the success will enjoy a positive momentum going into the next project or initiative. Being humble also means showing gratitude for the work and your relationships with your peers. Being a leader is a privilege, and humble leaders know this and act accordingly.

= underlying needs which unless to which drives positions

Know Their Needs

You will find it is easier to be good partner when you understand the needs and motivations of your fellow leadership team members. With this understanding, you will be in a position to anticipate needs, warn them of emerging problems, and share helpful ideas with peers. Leadership team members should be able to answer the following questions about each other:

- What are their needs? What are their strategic goals? What are their unique purposes in the organization and on this leadership team?

- What are their interests? What are their motivations? (These are often different from their needs.)

- What are their strengths and weaknesses? What unique skills and talents do they bring to the team and organization?

- What are their hot buttons? What frustrates them most?

- What do I expect from them? What do they expect from my department and me?

John and Barry were vice presidents reporting to the division president. They were both talented and opinionated. When together in meetings, their demeanor toward one another was cool, aloof, or confrontational. The real problem, however, came when they were not together. Both John and Barry took cheap shots at each other's expense in front of others. They also did not involve each other in decisions as often as they should have, preferring to avoid one another when possible. Barry was particularly critical and cynical of John and many of his group members. Neither was an inexperienced leader; they should have known better than to relate in this dysfunctional way. As if the poor relations between John and Barry were not enough, the managers who reported to them were beginning to emulate the dysfunction between them. The leadership team, too, was affected because their relationship got in the way of open and productive team dialogue. Both John and Barry had legitimate concerns that should have been debated by the leadership team, but their lack of partnership and clashing styles kept them from seeing or solving the problem. It took having a manager who worked for John and worked closely with Barry to call their attention to what was going on. To their credit, once they saw the impact their poor partnership was having on their results and their teams, they were able to become effective partners. In just a couple months, the improvement was significant, and both were realizing benefits in terms of productivity and worker satisfaction.

How would you assess the partnership between members of your leadership team? Use these partnering techniques to help you and your peers do your best work together. Partnership will make the leadership team stronger and more agile. When peers become advocates and coaches, they add value to each other's quests for results and efficiency. Effective partnerships are valuable assets for leadership team members. Great partners share ownership for projects and collectively work together to enjoy success and recover from failure.

Working on Your Teaming Skills

Your leadership team will have a better chance to meet its goals if you reduce leadership style clashes and increase partnership. How should you build teaming skills, given that you spend only about 5% of your time with your leadership team and have many goals to accomplish in this time? We recommend that you strengthen relationships and increase collaboration with every task the team takes on. For example:

- Incorporate partnership into meeting ground rules and discussion practices.
- Identify teaming expectations as part of your team definition of success.
- Assign two or more leadership team members as co-owners of key strategic initiatives to facilitate greater partnership and more frequent opportunities to collaborate.

• Get together for an informal gathering on a quarterly basis. Select an activity that will enable relationship building.

• Periodically talk about the benefits of modeling excellent teaming skills. All it takes is 5 to 10 minutes every few months to reinforce expectations and keep teaming top-of-mind.

• Hold team leadership team members accountable for being productive partners by including it as a performance indicator or an element within your performance indicators.

Talk about what great teaming looks like and why it is important. Leaders, like most employees, will rise to the level of expectations when they know what excellence looks like in action and align their daily practices to support performance. Leaders are leaders because they have the potential to transform people and groups for the better. Role modeling effective teaming skills is one way to reverberate excellence.

"Only by engaging can you influence. But engaging also means you will be influenced."[4]

—Peter Firestein

Endnotes

1. John Hope Bryant, *Love Leadership: The New Way to Lead in a Fear-Based World*, 30.

2. Marshall Goldsmith, *What Got You Here, Won't Get You There*, 45.

3. Tom Peters, *Fast Company* blog, February 28, 2001, www.fastcompany.com/magazine/44/rules.html?page=0%2C1.

4. Peter Firestein, *Crisis of Character: Building Corporate Reputation in the Age of Skepticism*, 17.

3

Meetings Are Money

"In many companies, meetings themselves are a source of distraction from higher-value work that people feel they could otherwise be doing."[1]

—Tony Schwartz

How often have you left a meeting room and thought—that was two hours of my life I will never get back? Our senior leadership team survey results reinforced what many of us have seen and felt: Meetings are often a waste of time. We asked survey participants to tell us what a fly would see if it observed their team discussions. The choices that received the *lowest* scores were

- Team members prepare well for team meetings.
- Meetings are well run and productive.
- Leadership styles do not clash within the team.
- Team members share the same priorities.
- Team members are candid with each other.
- Team members represent each other well.
- Team members look out for each other and don't let each other fail.

How would your team rate each other on the above behaviors? While the idea that some meetings are ineffective is not surprising, it is tragic and unacceptable. In this chapter, we make the case why we all should care a lot more about meeting effectiveness and share ways we can use leadership team meetings to create more value from our precious time.

Let's start by talking about costs. Meetings are very expensive, much more so than many leaders realize. One way we propose that you look at the cost of meetings might change the way you value your time. We created two indices you can use to assess the effectiveness of your meetings. The first is the Cost of Meetings Index, and the second is Value of Meetings Hurdle Index.

The Cost of Meetings Index

The Cost of Meetings Index is an estimated average of the salary and benefits costs associated with leadership meetings. See Table 3.1 for our estimates for small, medium, and large organizations. Because one of the practice areas for our consulting firm is compensation, we conduct and subscribe to many comprehensive salary surveys. We created the Cost of Meetings Index by averaging cash salaries for selected senior leadership positions across several surveys and separated the results into three buckets based on revenue amounts. This is an approximate calculation, for sure, but we think it offers a helpful and valid way to look at the cost of leadership team meetings. If you would like to create a more precise Cost of Meetings Index for your organization, see the sidebar to plug in your organization's salary and benefits numbers into our formula.

TABLE 3.1   The Cost of Meetings Index

Size of Organization	Average Cost of Meetings Per Leader, Per Hour
Small (up to $100 million in revenue/year)	$90
Medium ($101–$500 million in revenue/year)	$200
Large (over $500 million in revenue/year)	$350

Do these numbers surprise you? They shouldn't, but wait before you use these to determine the costs of your leadership team meetings. This calculation is just the first drop in the bucket.

Value of Meetings Hurdle

The Cost of Meetings Index is a good starting point but does not express the *opportunity costs* of meetings. Opportunity costs are much higher because they are equal to the value that a leader could generate if he or she were not busy in a meeting. It is an expression of how that time could be put to use if it were available. Opportunity costs are a bit tricky to calculate because they depend on the leader and the situation. Even so, we think it is important to consider opportunity costs and hold your leadership team meetings to a standard of effectiveness that considers what leaders could and should do with their time.

We considered several approaches for estimating opportunity costs and asked ourselves how to best estimate the average value that you hope each executive will generate for the organization. We started by thinking about typical financial investments and what might be considered a good return. Using a Wall Street metaphor, a 10% return on investment per year might be acceptable. Should opportunity costs be similarly evaluated? No. We don't think this point of view is adequate because we expect more than a 10% return on the financial investment we make in our executive's salaries and benefits.

Next we thought about the percent of revenue/sales model. Many organizations carry payroll costs that equal 30–60% of their top line revenue/sales. This ratio might suggest that the expected value in terms of top line revenue/sales of each salary dollar is twice its cost. We are getting closer to opportunity costs, but this is still much less than the value to expect from yourself and other leaders.

How about the consulting firm model? Consulting companies often set revenue goals for their practice leaders based on multipliers ranging from 2.5 to 4 times their salary. The limitation of this and the percent of revenue/sales metaphors is that they both capture only the value leaders generate related to revenue. Revenue is easily measurable, but it is not the only type of value that leaders generate for their organizations. In fact, most of the value a leader brings will manifest in less tangible ways before affecting top-line revenue/sales or bottom-line profits (losses). Here are a few examples of types of value we expect executives to generate beyond revenue generation:

- **Resource management**—How well people, processes, and capital are utilized.
- **Capacity building**—How well people and processes continuously grow and improve.
- **Culture, retention, and ownership**—The extent to which the environment catalyzes employee engagement, satisfaction, and focus.
- **Market and brand development**—How well the organization's reputation and brand is managed to enable success today and tomorrow.
- **Stakeholder confidence**—The extent to which leadership practices and relationships engender trust and confidence with key stakeholders.
- **Decision making**—How well and how quickly decisions are made that enable others to move forward.
- **Removal of barriers**—How barriers to progress are reduced, eliminated, and foreseen and prevented.
- **Risk leadership and management**—How potential opportunities and threats are assessed and managed.
- **Product, service, and program development**—How leaders improve the organization's offerings to the marketplace.
- **Strategic thinking**—Shaping the organization's future.
- **Setting the tone for excellence**—How leaders create a context for all employees about how things ought to work within the organization.

- **Relationships**—The strength and depth of relationships with employees at all levels and with other stakeholders.

These are just a few examples of the ways leaders ought to generate value for their organizations above and beyond—but ultimately enabling positive—financial results. Considering all these types of expected values, opportunity costs for time spent in meetings is quite high. It's reasonable to think about opportunity costs in terms of five or ten times actual salary and benefits costs. That said, we are using a very conservative three times salary and benefits costs for our Value of Meetings Hurdle Rate. This should be considered a *low* estimate. Your opportunity costs are likely much higher.

The Value of Meetings Hurdle Index, as displayed in Table 3.2, is the minimum value you ought to expect from the time you spend in meetings per person per hour. You can use this index to help shape, plan, and manage your meetings and improve their effectiveness.

TABLE 3.2 Cost of Meetings and Value of Meetings Index

Size Organization	Average Cost of Meetings per Leader, per Hour	Value of Meetings Hurdle Recommended Index (3 x cost) per Leader, per Hour
Small (up to $100 million in revenue/year)	$90	$270
Medium ($101–$500 million in revenue/year)	$200	$600
Large (over $500 million in revenue/year)	$350	$1,050

The numbers in Table 3.2 are useful to think about, but they might not seem compelling enough to you because they are expressed in terms of one hour and one executive. Can you imagine how these hours add up? Now that we have shared the Cost of Meetings and Value of Meetings indices, let's use these estimates on a few examples:

Example 1: Medium-sized organization, team of 10, two-hour monthly staff meeting.

Cost: $4,000 per month, $48,000 per year.

Value Hurdle: $12,000 per month, $144,000 per year.

Example 2: Division leadership team (using small organization numbers because division earns 50 million in revenue per year) of a large company. Seven leaders, one-hour meeting every Tuesday morning (in person or call in).

Cost: $630 per week, $32,670 per year.

Value Hurdle: $1,890 per week, $98,010 per year.

These are per meeting costs and don't tell the entire story of how the costs of various meetings add up. Let's also look at an estimate for the costs of meetings for all leaders each year. We worked with a hospital system that had 40 executives and 600 senior leaders. If we assume the medium-sized salary and benefits numbers for this organization, the system-wide cost for each meeting hour is $128,000. What is the yearly cost? To calculate the yearly cost of meetings, we need to make a few assumptions. In 2001, Nicholas Romano, Jr. and Jay Nunamaker, Jr. spoke at the International Conference on Systems Sciences about their analysis of how meetings impact business. Sourcing research conducted over the last 30 years, they reported that managers and leaders spend, on average, 50% or more of their time in meetings and that time spent in meetings is increasing each year. Assuming a conservative 40-hour workweek, or 20 hours spent in meetings per week per leader, the costs for meetings for this hospital system is at least $128,000,000 (assuming 20 hours per week for 50 weeks worked). And the opportunity costs? Using our Value of Meetings Hurdle Index, the opportunity costs are at least $384,000,000, and all these numbers are conservative estimates. The real costs are likely much higher.

Another way to look at yearly costs for a leadership team is to use our estimate that 5% of your time is spent together as a team. For a medium-sized organization with a leadership team of eight professionals, the costs of their 5% spent together is $166,400 and opportunity costs for this time is $499,200—a half million! This calculation, of course, is conservative and does not include any of other meetings leaders might attend on a weekly basis.

How to Create Your Own Cost of Meetings Index

Would you like to create your own Cost of Meetings Index? Plug the average yearly salary and benefits of your leadership team into the following formula:

Start by calculating the average yearly salary of each team member (total base salaries for team members divided by the number of members on the team) or an estimate of this number provided by the human resources leader).

Divide the average yearly salary by 2080 to get an average hourly rate for each leader.

Multiply the average hourly rate by 1.30 to add back in the cost of benefits.

The resulting number is your Cost of Meetings Index per leader, per hour.

To create your Value of Meetings Hurdle, multiply the Cost of Meetings Index by three (or the multiplier you choose based on the value you expect each leader to contribute to the organization).

Think about the value that you expect from leaders. When you hire a VP, what are you hoping his or her impact on the organization will be? If you have not thought about value of time in this way before, we urge you to give it a try because it will revolutionize your thinking on how you spend your time.

Have we gotten your attention? We hope so because the time you spend together is precious, costly, and ought to be valued as such. Are you worried that your meetings might not meet the Value of Meetings Hurdle? Excellent! This is the first step toward reinventing the time you spend with your peers. Leadership team meetings can and should be high-value activities. Here are several meeting outcomes that offer high value:

- **Building relationships**—As we discussed in detail in Chapter 2, "The Clash of Titans: Executive Teaming," how you and your peers lead together matters. If you have strong relationships, your meeting discourse will improve, and you will make better decisions as a team. Time spent building trust, mutual respect, and professional affection is highly valuable.

- **Making effective decisions**—When you and your peers spend time to deliberate options and agree on a decision, you enable the people who are waiting for your decision to focus and act. If your discussions are open and everyone offers their best thinking, decision-making is an important and high-value added activity for the leadership team.

- **Strategic thinking**—This may seem obvious, but many leadership teams struggle to think strategically and stay out of the day-to-day minutia. On our leadership team survey, 56% said they wanted to develop stronger strategic thinking skills. Strategic thinking is not something reserved for a once yearly retreat; you and your team have the opportunity to be strategic every time you meet. Defining and communicating strategies is a core function of any leadership team, even those who lead divisions within larger organizations.

- **Collaboration**—Perhaps the least utilized opportunity on this list, conversations that help build collaboration can be a great use of your leadership team meeting time. Try to dedicate a portion of every regular meeting to building collaboration between peers. One way to do this would be to take 20 minutes of each meeting to discuss and brainstorm a problem, opportunity, or challenge of one of the team members (rotate the opportunity so that everyone benefits). This practice also builds relationships, awareness, and shared goals.

- **Creative thinking**—Leaders are often so busy that they take little time to think together, but high-level creative thinking is very valuable. The brainpower in the average leadership team meeting is significant and should be tested, stretched, and used to improve their businesses. It is more common to find creative thinking has been delegated to a functional or cross-functional group who then reports their findings to the leadership team. This is fine and appropriate for many topics, but you should also encourage your team to periodically start the creative thinking process yourselves. The more you enjoy exploring possibilities together, the stronger your shared ownership and passion will be. It is energizing to be highly engaged in creative thinking, and taking the time to be creative allows executives to stay fresh and on top of their game.

- **Assessing and creating plans to improve culture and organization capacity**—In Chapter 4, "Culture Is the Context and Often the Answer," we discuss how leadership teams can shape culture and their work environment. This is one of the best levers leaders have for steering their organizations toward sustainable success. Leadership teams should discuss culture and create or polish plans for improvement quarterly.

- **Discussing team health, strength, and reputation**—(See Chapter 1, "Executive Team Execution," for the leadership team measurement dashboard.) Our leadership team survey revealed that most teams don't regularly think about and measure their team health and strength, but this is an important and high-value added activity. The leadership team sets the tone for what it means and looks like to work well together. If something is important, it deserves to be measured and improved.

- **Discussing and agreeing on ways to connect with employees at all levels of the organization**—In Chapter 8, "Leadership Team Strategies for Remaining Union-Free," we make the case that this activity—connecting with employees at all levels—is an important success factor for remaining union-free. Even if unionization is not a concern for you, the broader point is that when frontline employees feel like they know, can trust, and feel connected with their organization's senior leaders, they demonstrate a higher comfort level with management and leadership in general. And this is a very good thing that improves ownership, engagement, and daily problem solving. By being visible and known, you make it easier for middle managers to implement your strategic intentions.

- **Leadership team member skill development**—As you will read in Chapter 6, "Getting Better Together," a leadership team can be well-positioned to help its members develop and grow as professionals, and your organization's success depends on you and your peers building the skills and habits you need to do your best work.

- **Enlivening and reengaging your commitment and dedication to the business, mission, and employees**—The energy that you and your peers have for the business will imbue the organization with a positive vibe and inspirational oomph. Do your leadership team meetings energize or drain you? They *can* and should be catalytic.

These are just a few of the high-value added ways to use your leadership team meeting time. These discussions share several characteristics including that they strengthen the team, improve focus, and move the work forward. To ensure that your meetings are a great use of your time, you will also want to improve the quality and effectiveness of the meeting process and conversations. Having an agenda packed with high-value added goals is a good start, but if the meetings don't fulfill these lofty goals, your great intentions will not yield adequate results. As we mentioned at the beginning of this chapter, our senior leadership team survey results showed that many leaders feel dissatisfied with how well leaders prepare for meetings and overall effectiveness of the time spent in meetings together.

"Focusing on contribution turns one of the inherent weaknesses of the executive's situation—his dependence on other people, his being within the organization—into a source of strength. It creates a team."[2]

—Peter Drucker, from *The Effective Executive*

Use ground rules to add helpful structure to your meetings. In *The Skilled Facilitator*, author Roger Schwarz spoke to the value of good ground rules:

The ground rules serve several functions. First, they are a diagnostic tool. By understanding the ground rules, you can quickly identify dysfunctional group behavior, which is inconsistent with the ground rules, so that you can intervene on it. Second, the ground rules are a teaching tool for developing effective group norms.[3]

We agree and find that ground rules can help you improve meeting dialogue and outcomes. And because the cost of leadership team meetings is so high, we recommend you use special ground rules. The ground rules we use are not the same as the standard list you can get by Googling "meeting ground rules" or that are offered up in meeting facilitation training classes. Because the Value of Meetings Hurdle is very high, your meeting ground rules need to enable a higher level of results. We call these amped-up agreements "X-Factor Meeting Ground Rules" because they will help you and your peers bring out the best in your conversations and tap into the additive value of catalytic executive discourse. The following contrasts common meeting ground rules and our list. Some X-Factor Meeting Ground Rules are more rigorous versions of the more common variety while others are unique and needed to create a higher level of meetings value and results.

- **Common Meeting Ground Rule:** Everyone participates.

  X-Factor Meeting Ground Rule: Participation is not an option, nor is it an invitation to grandstand or overparticipate. Every executive is expected to participate in team discussions in ways that moves the conversation forward. Each executive is also expected to help bring out the best thinking in his or her peers. If participation is not strong and focused, it is a team failure.

- **Common Meeting Ground Rule:** All ideas are welcome.

  X-Factor Meeting Ground Rule: Share relevant information in ways that will be heard and understood. Your candor about concerns, worries, reservations, and ideas is important and required.

- **Common Meeting Ground Rule:** Disagree in private, not in public.

  X-Factor Meeting Ground Rule: Discuss and agree on communication plans. Your meeting outcomes can be of value only when others in the organization understand how decisions and strategies impact them and your expectations for next steps and measure for success. Each issue resolved in a leadership team meeting should have corresponding agreements about how and when the information will be communicated and managed.

- **Common Meeting Ground Rule:** Silence is the same thing as agreement.

  X-Factor Meeting Ground Rule: Meetings are where leadership and management occur and are the primary tool the team has for creating common understanding and leading the organization forward. The effectiveness of meetings, therefore, is of paramount importance to all leadership team members, and this shows in how they model productive meeting and teaming skills.

- **Common Meeting Ground Rule:** Don't hold side conversations or text or email during the meeting and silence phones.

  X-Factor Meeting Ground Rule: Don't tolerate low-value added conversations. If you do not see the worth or value of a leadership team meeting discussion, it is your responsibility to address this concern with the group. It is not acceptable to become distracted or disconnected from a conversation—be proactive in fixing the situation.

- **Common Meeting Ground Rule:** Arrive on time and end on time.

  X-Factor Meeting Ground Rule: Time is precious and expensive; don't waste yours or your peers'. Every moment that the team is waiting for late attendees represents thousands of dollars wasted. Get the meeting started on time regardless of who is missing or disband and reschedule the meeting if a quorum is not present. Late or absent participants are expected to support and represent the decisions made by the quorum.

- **Common Meeting Ground Rule:** Use an agenda and goals for all meetings.

  X-Factor Meeting Ground Rule: Meeting agenda items and goals should have the potential for meeting or exceeding the Value of Meetings Hurdle rate. Other proposed agenda items should be handled in more economical methods, delegated, or eliminated.

- **Common Meeting Ground Rule:** Prepare for meetings.

  X-Factor Meeting Ground Rule: Every meeting will have mandatory prework and preparation. The time a leadership team spends together will be of greater value when all team members take sufficient time to prepare. Meeting leaders or designees should define the prework and preparation that will best enhance meeting discussions and desired outcomes.

- **Common Meeting Ground Rule:** Keep discussion on-topic and focused.

  X-Factor Meeting Ground Rule: Focus on the quality of conversations. While every meeting has a desired focus and goals, the quality of the dialogue (which leads to better thinking, actions, and results) is most important. This may mean that some discussions will take longer than expected, and others can be quickly concluded.

- **Common Meeting Ground Rule:** Follow through on agreements and action items.

  X-Factor Meeting Ground Rule: Preparing for meetings and completing assigned action items is a core function of each leader's job. A failure to meet these requirements will constitute a performance issue and could result in career consequences. The cost of meetings requires a high level of results orientation.

- **Common Meeting Ground Rule:** Treat confidential information and conversations appropriately.

  X-Factor Meeting Ground Rule: Meeting outcomes shall be communicated in one consistent voice. It is not acceptable for leaders to share the nature of disagreements discussed in meetings, and it is never okay to bad mouth peers. It is the team's responsibility to represent each other well at all times because a division at the top becomes a gorge of dysfunction at lower levels in the organization.

- **Common Meeting Ground Rule:** Focus on intent, not positions, and don't take cheap shots.

  X-Factor Meeting Ground Rule: Demonstrate respect, trust, and care for each other, even when discussing diverse ideas. Strained or unproductive relationships wreck the quality of the leadership team thinking, actions, and ultimately, results. Leaders are expected to work well with all team members and not let differences in style clash and get in the way of the team's results.

- **Common Meeting Ground Rule:** Listen well.

  X-Factor Meeting Ground Rule: Bring your best energy and passion to each meeting. An energized and engaged leadership team will imbue the entire organization with a high-velocity vibe that will impact how everyone approaches their work. Be the culture and disposition you hope to see at lower levels of the organization.

- **Common Meeting Ground Rule:** Support team decisions as if they are your own.

  X-Factor Meeting Ground Rule: Model agility and good change leadership. Your organization's capacity for change begins with how their leaders lead, communicate, and manage change. Your leadership team will be making decisions that create change, and it is important that your meeting discussions demonstrate agility and best practices for how to implement changes. Be cognizant of the "marathon effect" and that you are farther along in understanding and accepting each change than the folks who you will rely on to make changes the new norm.

- **Common Meeting Ground Rule:** Meeting participants should feel good about the meeting and the part they played in the conversation.

  X-Factor Meeting Ground Rule: Ignite passion and commitment. Every leadership team meeting should engage team members such that they are more energized and focused when they leave the meeting room than when they came into it—even if the topic is serious or troublesome (like solving a tough problem).

Our X-Factor Meeting Ground Rules may seem a bit tough-minded, and they intentionally are that way because of the valuable nature of your meetings. Imagine what your meetings would look and feel like if all team members followed these results-oriented and hard-hitting ground rules! We feel strongly that all leaders will be well-served when they hold themselves and their peers to a high standard for meeting effectiveness. It must be a team effort and not something left to relying on individuals doing their part. If a meeting gets off track, it is not just their time being wasted—it is yours, too.

"Don't talk unless you can improve the silence."
—Proverb

Talking Beyond the Point of Contribution

As a leader who has risen to a position of immense responsibility and scope, you likely have been positively reinforced for showing leadership during team meetings, departmental communications, and daily gatherings. We have observed that some leaders seem to equate speaking with leadership, and they talk on and on to the point where others are thinking about what they are going to have for lunch if this meeting ever ends. There is an art to knowing how much to say so that you are clear and helpful, but don't talk beyond the point of contribution. Given the high cost of leadership team meetings, communicating fully while being concise is critical.

Most leaders never receive training or coaching on this topic, and yet over-communicators are a major source of aggravation and frustration for those who must endure through these mini-monologues. We worked with one organization that had something called "Tim Time." When Tim was going to be at the meeting, they padded the meeting agenda because they knew he would likely talk too much and cause the meeting to run over time. You do not want to be like Tim, and it is not just an inconvenience—it is unprofessional and irresponsible. Period. Here are a few tips to help you improve the quality and conciseness of your meeting participation:

- **Plan ahead**—Write down your thoughts ahead of time and create a list of talking points. Stick to those talking points unless someone asks for further clarification.

- **Monitor the volume of your comments**—We know the aforementioned Tim, and he did not fully realize how many times he chimed in during each meeting. Write a small check on your note pad each time you are about to speak.

- **Ask more questions**—Most over-communicators offer many opinions and tell lots of stories—some stories more than once. If you ask more questions, you will engage others and help improve the quality of the discussion.

- **Check in with people**—Make it a habit to check for understanding because the most common complaint we hear is that over-communicators make great points, but they don't stop and often repeat themselves. Ask, "Is that clear, or do you want more detail?" or "Have I gone on too long?"

- **Care enough to ask for peer coaching**—If you are an over-communicator, your peers know this. Ask them whether you have a habit of talking beyond the point of contribution. Tell them you want to know the truth and that they do not need to sugar-coat it. If they tell you that this is an issue, take in the information and thank them. Whatever you do, don't go into a long explanation of why you think you do this or defend yourself because this would be the quickest way to demonstrate that you are not listening!

- **If overtalkers reduce your meeting effectiveness, use a digital timer**—This approach should be used to help improve self-awareness about how long they drone on but should not get in the way of the team engaging in meaty discussions.

Why Are You Meeting?

In addition to using our X-Factor Meeting Ground Rules, we would invite you to question why you are meeting in the first place. Many staff meetings, even those with C-level execs are held out of routine and fail to meet the hurdle for either real or opportunity costs. To get the most out of your meetings, consider doing the following:

- Mess with the meeting times. Try cutting the length of your meetings by half and observe how much less is accomplished. Often, you will get the same amount done, and this should tell you that your agendas are weak. Use the "found" time to add more value (see the list offered earlier in this chapter).

- Rotate meeting leadership and focus. Give each leadership team member a turn at planning, leading, and facilitating the meeting. Give each person the same guideline: Plan and conduct a meeting that is a great use of our time together. Encourage massive reinventions and wild ideas.

- Do five-minute post-mortems on every meeting before you adjourn. Ask, "How did we do using this time to add value and energize our leadership?"

- For topics that are not confidential, videotape your meetings and share them with your employees. Or share a portion of the meeting. Or do a five-minute video recap of the meeting at the end for your employees. Or invite a few employees into each meeting to observe. Would your behavior change if you thought your employees were watching? We know there is value in allowing you to build relationships in private and be very open about topics that might cause surprise or stress to your employees if they heard them. Even so, think about how you can share some aspect of your meetings with your employees as doing so will accomplish two goals. First, your employees will get to know you better and trust leadership more, and second, it will improve your meeting time effectiveness.

- Find ways to generate energy during meetings. Stand up and do stretches (great for safety) during the meeting. Talk about important topics and avoid going down unproductive rabbit holes. Serve fresh fruit and espresso. Do some creative work, even if just for five minutes, at every meeting. Interview one frontline level employee for ten minutes of every meeting to learn about them and their work and what advice they have for how leaders can make yours a better place to work (win-win again).

- Ask someone from the OD (organization development) or training departments to facilitate your meetings. With the cost of meetings as high as it is, it is well worth the investment in a professional facilitator. Let the facilitator know that you want to ensure meetings meet high expectations for value, relationship building, and dialogue quality. If you talk about confidential topics, you should be able to find an OD person that can be trusted to keep meeting discussions private.

Do you use a facilitator or ask the OD department to help team members work better together? Here is another example from a colleague of ours, Connie Kocher, an OD leader of a multiplant manufacturer:

> Many organizations use an OD tool called New Manager Assimilation. We also use this intervention with new members to the Executive Team to get them past the initial rituals of accepting a new member to the team. This facilitated discussion allows the existing team members and the new member get their agendas, concerns, and uncertainties right out on the table and upfront. This establishes good rapport and a foundation for understanding and thus collaboration going forward.

Helping with team assimilation is a great idea. Do any of these ideas look like they would be of benefit to you and your fellow team members? Our point it this: Do something. Don't tolerate meetings that are not a great use of your time. Lisa recalls a time when she was facilitating an executive strategic planning meeting. This leadership team consisted of a president and six direct reports, and they together ran a small but well-regarded travel company that generated about 55 million dollars in revenue each year. During the two-day strategic planning session, one of the VPs mentioned that their weekly staff meeting often felt like a waste of time. Lisa asked the others if they felt the same, and all of them did, even the president. Because we had done a lot of work with this team and had a strong and candid relationship with them, Lisa said, "Are you kidding me? Each week you spend time together that you all think is a waste of time? Why are you doing this?" Team members agreed that they were just going through the motions. After discussing the cost of meetings and the obligation to add value, the team agreed that they would never again tolerate a bad staff meeting and that they each had the responsibility to stop any future meeting that did not seem like it was adding enough value. These were all smart, hard-working executives who had gotten caught up in a routine that no one thought was working for them. Unfortunately, this scenario is very common.

Meetings are money, but we often don't think of them in this way. We have seen brilliant—crazy brilliant—executives be totally clueless when it comes to spending meeting time wisely. It is common, so don't beat yourself up about it if you have not done enough to ensure effective meetings in the past. Leadership team meetings can and should be excellent tools for driving forward organizational success and results. With a good focus and proper reverence of meetings, you can ensure that the time your team spends together enhances progress and strategic implementation. Never lament about time wasted in meetings again!

"If, as it appears, automatic consistency functions as a shield against thought, it should not be surprising that such consistency can also be exploited by those who prefer that we respond to their requests without thinking. For the profiteers, whose interests will be served by an unthinking, mechanical reaction to their requests, our tendency for automatic consistency is a gold mine."[4]

—Robert Cialdini

Endnotes

1. Tony Schwartz, *The Way We're Working Isn't Working: The Four Forgotten Needs That Energize Great Performance*, 223.

2. Peter Drucker, *The Effective Executive*, 66.

3. Roger Schwarz, *The Skilled Facilitator: A Comprehensive Resource for Consultants, Facilitators, Managers, Trainers and Coaches*, 10.

4. Robert Cialdini, *Influence: Science and Practice*, 58.

4

Culture Is the Context and Often the Answer

"I couldn't have laid out a strategy that would have led to the partnerships that the orchids have made real. I couldn't have mustered the cleverness and foresight to look into the future and see these things as goals. But my point is, I didn't have to. All I had to do was trust my intuition that there was something powerful in the beauty of a flower."[1]
—Bill Strickland

Many of our clients are fascinated by the topic of culture, and we can understand why. Your organization's culture can either enable or get in the way of strategic implementation and positive results. Every organization has a culture, but many leadership teams do little to proactively shape it to support important goals. If you have ever lead a company turnaround, you likely know that aligning the culture to match new strategies and intentions is hard work but critical. In this chapter, we explore what culture is, how leadership teams create culture, how to change culture, and how a strong culture supports organizational success.

According to an interview he did with the CEO Forum Group in 2004, Heinz Australia CEO Peter Widdows credits their cultural change for their improvement in revenues and profitability and retention. The need for deep cultural changes was apparent to Widdows:

People think culture is a very wooly kind of issue, but as I examined the business after taking up my appointment last year, I became more and more convinced that the culture was the biggest problem the business faced.[2]

Peter Widdows noticed that his was a work environment where innovation and creativity were repressed and knew he needed to change this for the company to be successful after years of decline. DaVita's CEO Kent Thiry had significant concerns about his organization's culture when he accepted the CEO job, too. In the May/June issue of *Chief Executive*, he teed up the challenge:

It was quite an alienated place to work because it was technically bankrupt and sued by shareholders and investigated by the SEC. People were angry because the previous CEO had taken a lot of money out of the company. Morale had imploded. People were angry, alienated, scared, and depressed.[3]

Leadership teams can improve culture, and they sometimes tear it down. Zappos is famous for having a positive and productive culture, but in a January 2010 *New York Times* article, CEO Tony Hsieh recalled a time when, before joining Zappos, he and his leadership team wrecked a company culture—a situation that he credits as a major motivation for selling the company to Microsoft:

From the outside, it looked like it was a great acquisition, $265 million, but most people don't know the real reason why we ended up selling the company. It was because the company culture just went completely downhill. When it was starting out, when it was just 5 or 10 of us, it was like your typical dot-com...By the time we got to 100 people, even through we hired people with the right skill sets and experiences, I just dreaded getting out of bed in the morning and was hitting the snooze button over and over.[4]

Hsieh went on to say that he realized that if he didn't want to come to work, his employees likely felt the same. This failure was top of mind when he joined Zappos, and it drove him to take a different and more proactive approach to shaping and maintaining a positive organizational culture there. A poor culture is easy to see, and it feels oppressive and draining.

We return to these examples from Heinz Australia, DaVita, and Zappos, and others as the chapter unfolds. When we call something a healthy culture, we are describing a work environment that represents an organization's mission, vision, values, and intentions and that enables and catalyzes people to do their best work. Improving an organization's success through aligning its culture became a popular focus of work in the 1980s. During this time, many behavioral science researchers studied and acknowledged the power and importance of organizational culture. In the last 30 years, organizational culture has become a regular consideration during strategic planning sessions and throughout change management initiatives. Building culture starts with an understanding of how it is created and then how to change it. Let's start with attempting a definition of organizational culture.

What Is an Organization's Culture?

We found several definitions of organizational culture. A frequently cited definition comes from organization development pioneer Edgar Schein. In his book, *Organizational Culture and Leadership*, Schein described culture as being deeper than behaviors and artifacts:

> I will argue that the term "culture" should be reserved for the deeper level of basic assumptions and beliefs that are shared by members of an organization, that operate unconsciously, and that define in a basic "taken for granted" fashion an organization's view of itself and its environment.[5]

Schein emphasized assumptions and beliefs while others see culture as a product of values. In *Culture's Consequences*, Geert Hofstede wrote, "I treat culture as 'the collective programming of the mind which distinguishes the members of one human group from another.' ... Culture, in this sense, includes systems of values; and values are among the building blocks of culture. Culture is to a human collectively what personality is to an individual."[6]

Beliefs and values are linked. What about understanding? In her article, "Organizations as Culture-Bearing Milieux," Meryl Reis Louis wrote that "any social group, to the extent that it is a distinctive unit, will have some degree of culture differing from that of other groups, a somewhat different set of common understandings around which action is organized, and these differences will find expression in a language whose nuances are peculiar to that group."[7] These three descriptions of organization culture find root in collectively held individual thinking processes.

In their piece titled, "The Role of Symbolic Management," Caren Siehl and Joanne Martin argued that "culture consists of three components: context, forms, and strategies."[8] This description suggests a more systemic description of culture with both internal and external components. In *Riding the Waves of Culture*, Fons Trompenaars offers another systemic model and describes three levels of culture: 1) the explicit layer made up of artifacts and products and other observable signs, 2) the middle layer of norms and values, and 3) the implicit layer, which is comprised of basic assumptions and beliefs.[9] In *Corporate Culture and Performance*, John Kotter and James Heskett acknowledge internal and external components of culture, too. They see organizational culture as having "two levels, which differ in their visibility and resistance to change."[10] The invisible level is made up of shared values that tend to persist over time and are harder to change. The visible level of culture includes group behaviors and actions, which are easier to change.

Is it important or even possible to sort out these definitions and decide which is most accurate? Schein, for example, argued that artifacts and products "reflect the organization's culture, but none of them is the essence of culture."[11] The differences and interconnectedness of assumptions, beliefs, understanding, and values could be studied further to determine which are more elemental to culture, but would that be time well spent? Which is most important, that a definition be right or that it be helpful? Although we cannot determine the right definition, each of these descriptions adds value to our approach to strengthening organizational culture. Based on the work of these and other researchers, we could make the following conclusions:

- Each company has a unique culture that changes over time.
- Beliefs, assumptions, values, and understanding—and the actions and norms they produce—are important components of culture.
- We recognize culture by observing actions and artifacts (explicit factors).
- While some call it a subculture and others a climate within the larger culture, there may be cultural differences within subgroups of an organization.
- Observable behaviors and actions are easier to change than are beliefs and values.
- The observable elements of culture affect the invisible elements and vice versa. Change in one cultural element will impact other elements.

Although not apparent in these definitions, it is also important to consider how cultures external to the organization impact and affect the organization's culture. For example, a silicon chip manufacturing plant in Portland, Oregon, may employ workers from different cultures than would plants in New Mexico, South Carolina, or Delhi, India. A strong internal culture will be enriched by the employees' diverse individual backgrounds.

We would be remiss if we did not also mention how the internal culture is impacted by the organization's external brand and vice versa. Some leaders refer to this as their internal brand, which is a part of the overall organization's culture. In a December 2009 *BusinessWeek* article, writer Steve McKee discussed a recent move that Starbucks made to try and realign its internal brand with its external brand. They acknowledged through several heart-wrenching press releases and statements that they had grown so fast that they had forgotten their core mission—to create a special and unique customer experience. Starbucks shut down their 7,100 company-owned stores for two hours to conduct customer service training:

> Some cynics called it a publicity stunt, but I think it was a sincere initiative from a company that has long demonstrated a commitment to helping its employees live the brand. Starbucks' bold, store-closing move was about more than training and free press; it was a potent form of internal branding. Closing the stores sent an unmistakable message that Schultz was serious about his expectations that all 135,000 Starbucks employees deliver on the brand promise.[12]

McKee defined an internal brand as "having a continuous process in place by which you ensure your employees understand the "who" and "why" behind your business proposition."[13] The internal brand is an important cultural element and can get in the way of change if not consistent with the external brand. Peter Widdows focused on creating an internal brand consistent with his external brand at Heinz Australia:

> I think there is a really important issue here—consistency between the internal organizational environment and the quality of the brands and products you want to make and market. I think it's difficult to generate excitement around brands and products if the organization itself is pessimistic and defeatist.[14]

We have a client who recently changed their strategy to be more consumer-centric. They created a marketing and sales strategic plan that supported their goals, but after a year, they realized that how people worked, collaborated, and made decisions had changed little. If you were a fly on the wall inside the organization, you would never guess that they were trying to be consumer-centric. This is the point of culture realignment—to manifest the strategies and intentions of your organization. The internal brand is a part of the culture and an important consideration for all leadership teams.

Employees sense their organization's culture soon after they join the company. They might have a hard time describing the culture, but they know it when they feel it. Each culture will have desirable and undesirable elements (which might be assessed differently depending on your point of view or position within the organization). There may be similarities in particular industries or regions (startups are fast-paced, high-tech companies feel creative, Seattle-based companies are more relaxed), but each company will have unique cultural attributes.

How Are Organizational Cultures Formed and Changed?

Organizational culture is socially constructed—it is created and changed through conversation. Each conversation makes meaning of observable actions and reinforces, builds upon, or challenges the current cultural norms and beliefs. The concept of social construction of organizational culture is vital for leadership teams, offers them an opportunity, and poses two challenges. The opportunity is that if you change the right conversations, you can change the culture for the better. The challenges you should consider are that 1) if you don't change the conversations, the culture will not change and 2) conversations that do not support the desired changes will make progress doubly hard to achieve.

Edgar Schein believed that leaders, through their daily conversations, created and changed culture. Here is another quote from *Organizational Culture and Leadership*:

> Organizational cultures are created by leaders, and one of the most decisive functions of leadership may well be the creation, the management, and—if and when that may become necessary—the destruction of culture.[15]

It is through conversation (talk, observed actions, listening, writing) that leadership teams manage, reinforce and create culture. Leadership is a social act, and a leader's greatest tool for shaping culture is workplace communication. Culture change will gain more velocity when the entire leadership team is driving the culture in the same direction. The opposite is also true. If one or more leadership team member does not model and support the desired culture change, he or she will undermine, endanger, and may inhibit progress.

Kent Thiry of DaVita recognized the power of conversation to build culture and used communication as a tool for creating understanding and commitment:

> We learned that if you state the intent out loud, most people feel a huge obligation to do what they say; and, therefore, if you get people to talk about ideals or values or a mission out loud, they're far more likely to want to pursue it.[16]

Our experience supports the idea that conversations are a leadership team's currency for creating change and ensuring focus. A single conversation does not change a culture—it could not—because culture is developed over time. Many consistent conversations, delivered by all leadership team members and then others in the organization, are needed to nudge a lumbering culture to a new place.

In our Senior Leadership Team Survey, we asked participants to indicate whether their teams discussed culture and whether they did anything to improve it. We asked each survey taker to select which one of these statement best described his team's practices (with percentages of responses):

- We regularly discuss how the organization's culture ought to change and put practices in place to facilitate its change. (43%)
- We talk about the organization's culture and believe it is strong and aligned with our strategies. (31%)
- We have talked about the organization's culture, believe it should change, but have not done anything to change it. (21%)
- We have not talked about the organization's culture in the last year. (5%)

We were pleased to see that 95% of all executives reported that their teams have talked about organizational culture and that 43% report being proactive about improving culture. What the summary statistics don't show, however, is that the majority of teams disagreed about the role their team is taking regarding organizational culture. It was not uncommon to see a team of ten executives split between all four response options. The variety of responses to this question makes us wonder whether organizational culture holds its proper place as a specific and regular leadership team topic and part of every strategic planning discussion. Once yearly conversations about culture at a leadership team retreat is not enough—not by a long shot.

The old adage goes something like this: How do you eat an elephant? Answer: One bite at a time. To change a culture, leadership teams must together engage in many conversations, one conversation at a time, time and time again.

Improving the Organization's Culture

A workplace culture can enable or hinder success. Culture is socially constructed, and leaders need to initiate conversations that tie cultural norms to the organization's goals. If the current culture is not in alignment with the new reality, leadership teams need to be the catalysts, or bridges, which create new understanding and help individuals select new behaviors and beliefs. Leadership teams should also define, clarify, and reinforce understanding of the actions and beliefs that build the desired culture.

Every senior team we have worked with has had big plans for their enterprises. That's why leaders exist, after all—to drive success forward. You don't want to maintain things, right? You want to help lead your organization to a better future. What impact do you want your leadership to have? Better results, a higher percentage of profit, revenue growth, a higher market share, new products and services, or world-class customer loyalty? Leadership teams that assess their culture as part of the strategic planning process will be better prepared to determine and implement the cultural changes that will best support the desired state.

Implementing one large change will be a challenge and might call for cultural realignment, but what happens when you are trying to make multiple changes? Nonstop change is common, and many organizations are struggling to keep up. Leaders layer initiatives onto already stressed people and systems, making it difficult for your improvements to take hold and work. We have seen this happen with many of our clients, and their employees can't keep up. What *should* be a set of well-positioned strategies becomes a shotgun blast of top-down adjustments that cause employee stress, confusion, and discomfort. When we work with companies to help them implement large-scale changes, we do a Capacity for Change assessment (C4C). This assessment tells leadership teams if their organizations are capable of making the changes they seek. Most of the time, the assessment results are disappointing. We have had leaders respond to the assessment results by saying that they need to change anyway and that their organization's' success depends upon it. Our answer to this response might seem a bit strong, but we find these leaders could benefit from a more reality-based point of view. You can say that the strategy is mission-critical all you want, but if your organization can't handle the changes, you will waste millions of dollars and immeasurable man-hours. You will feel like you are swimming through hardening cement. We know that change is important, and we think anything is possible *if* and *when* leadership teams get on board together to create an aligned, change-ready culture. If the culture is nimble (in the habit of being realigned), change efforts will be more fluid and effective.

Improving your organizational culture involves four repeating processes that serve to continually tune up the alignment of your culture to organizational values and strategies. And because culture changes a bit at a time, the four processes will best serve your goals when you and your team explore each of them regularly.

Figure 4.1 shows how the four processes interrelate. Once you get into the model, you keep going, revisiting each process when needed. When using the processes for the first time, you will want to go in the following order:

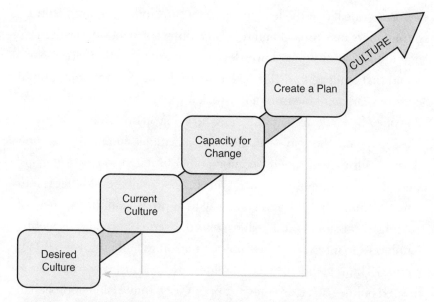

Figure 4.1   Steps leaders take to assess and build their desired organizational culture

1. Define the Desired Culture
2. Define Current Culture
3. Assess Capacity for Change
4. Create Plan for Cultural Improvement

Define the Desired Culture

Your desired culture should support today's and tomorrow's strategic initiatives and the reputation you want to create with customers and stakeholders. Some aspects of your desired culture may endure year after year, and some will need to adapt as your business changes. For example, we work with a high-tech client that has never been profitable. When the company was formed, profitability was not the top concern for the leadership team, who focused on building products, services, and market share. After several years, their need to turn a profit grew, and everyone on the management team was asked to focus on fiscal performance. The desired culture should mirror changes in the business's life cycle.

It is critical that the leadership team agree on the desired culture, or members may project and reinforce different values that will cause operational confusion at lower levels in the organization. We recommend that leadership teams take time to define/redefine the desired culture yearly and measure and tweak it quarterly as needed. So how do you define a desired culture, and how do you describe it? The simplest way and the way that most organizations communicate their desired culture is through a combination of their vision, mission, and values. You might not have made this connection before—that values equal culture—but this is a good way to approach culture. Instead of creating a mission, vision, values, *and* desired culture and expecting employees to internalize their unique meanings and uses, keep things simple. Think about it; if your values are not an expression of the desired culture, what are they? Zappos CEO Tony Hsieh approached redefining the desired culture by creating a focused list of core values:

> We formalized the definition of our culture into 10 core values. We wanted to come up with committable core values, meaning that we would actually be willing to hire and fire people based on those values, regardless of their individual job performance.[17]

We love Hsieh's comment about being willing to make decisions based on the core values; it is an important characteristic of a well-defined desired culture. How many times have you seen or experienced workplace cultures that bared little resemblance to the mission, vision, or values printed and on display in hallways, customer reception areas, and meeting rooms? It is better to have a smaller list of desired cultural elements that you are willing to manage to than it is to have a longer list that you cannot model and reinforce and that becomes little more than a flowery marketing statement.

Let's take a look at the mission, vision, and/or values of several well-known companies, starting with Zappos, as found on their corporate websites. As you read over each list, put a star by each cultural element that you think might also be important to your organization.

Zappos' 10 Core Values*

1. Deliver WOW Through Service

2. Embrace and Drive Change

3. Create Fun and a Little Weirdness

4. Be Adventurous, Creative, and Open-Minded

5. Pursue Growth and Learning

6. Build Open and Honest Relationships With Communication

7. Build a Positive Team and Family Spirit

8. Do More With Less

9. Be Passionate and Determined

10. Be Humble

*Source: www.zappos.com

DaVita's Mission and Values*

Our Mission: To be the Provider, Partner and Employer of Choice. We are becoming the greatest dialysis company the world has ever seen through our commitment to upholding our Mission and Values every day, in everything we do.

Our Values:

- **Service Excellence:** Serving others—our reason for existing. We continually seek to understand the needs of those who depend on us (our patients, doctors, and our fellow team members) and then to exceed their expectations.

- **Integrity:** We say what we believe, and we do what we say. We are trusted because we are trustworthy. In our personal, team, and organizational values, we strive for alignment in what we say and do.

- **Team:** One for All, and All for One! We work together, sharing a common purpose, a common culture, and common goals. We genuinely care for and support, not only those to whom we provide care, but those with whom we work shoulder-to-shoulder. We work together to pursue achieving our Mission.

- **Continuous Improvement:** We never stand still; we are never satisfied. Individually, and as teams, we constantly look at what we do and ask, "How can we do this better?" Then we use a systematic approach to take action.

- **Accountability:** We don't say, "It's not my fault," or "It's not my job." We take responsibility for meeting our commitments—our personal ones as well as those of the entire organization. We take ownership of the results.

- **Fulfillment:** We make a difference. We feel rewarded—personally and as a team—because what we do in our jobs is consistent with our goals and dreams. We believe "You must be the change you wish to see in the world" (Mahatma Gandhi). And, when you are the change, that's fulfilling!

- **Fun:** We enjoy what we do. We know kidney dialysis is hard work, but even hard work can be fun. We take our jobs seriously, but we feel a fun environment delivers better care to our patients while creating a better work environment for our teammates. We strive for excellence, and we have fun.

*Source: www.DaVita.com

Heinz Australia's Culture*

Heinz is an active and responsible member in its community.

- Like any citizen, we recognize the responsibility we have to supporting others within our own communities.

- Heinz employees take great pride in the activities we undertake to support our communities at both the local level through Help@hand and our volunteering efforts, and at a more national level through charity and emergency aid support, environmental activities, sponsorship, and scholarships.

Heinz is a "Great Place to Work."

The Heinz Australia business has undergone a transformation in the past few years, which has helped generate the success we are now enjoying. The culture that prevails within our company is an important enabler in maintaining and building on that success. It is simple but clear—we strive to make Heinz "A Great Place to Work." What that means to us is

- **Great Results:** Being a part of something successful. It takes the following points to make this happen.

- **Great Brands and Products:** Feeling proud of your work and the company you work for. Heinz products and brands are well-recognized and trusted for quality and nutrition.

- **Great People:** Working with and being inspired by excellent colleagues. Fast Moving Consumer Goods businesses attract passionate people.

- **Great Culture:** Being encouraged to do well and rewarded for effort. We relish the challenges our roles afford us in a supportive and fairly relaxed environment. It's a family-friendly workplace with a host of benefits that prove that a well-rounded lifestyle is valued here. Performance bonuses, paid parental leave, volunteer leave, fresh fruit, subsidized gym benefits, health and well-being programs, discounted stock purchase plans, free life and accident insurance, just to name just a few.

*Source: www.heinz.com.au

Amazon.com's Core Values*

- **Customer Obsession:** We start with the customer and work backward.

- **Innovation:** If you don't listen to your customers you will fail. But if you only listen to your customers you will also fail.

- **Bias for Action:** We live in a time of unheralded revolution and insurmountable opportunity—provided we make every minute count.

- **Ownership:** Ownership matters when you're building a great company. Owners think long-term, plead passionately for their projects and ideas, and are empowered to respectfully challenge decisions.

- **High Hiring Bar:** When making a hiring decision we ask ourselves: "Will I admire this person? Will I learn from this person? Is this person a superstar?"

- **Frugality:** We spend money on things that really matter and believe that frugality breeds resourcefulness, self-sufficiency, and invention!

*Source: www.amazon.com

MedCentral Health System's Mission, Vision, Pillars, and Values*

Mission: MedCentral Health System will provide expert care to the people of North Central Ohio.

Vision: MedCentral will be a recognized leader in health care quality.

Pillars:

- **Teamwork:** All of us at MedCentral will work together to provide the best care possible.

- **Quality:** MedCentral will be known for excellence in all that we do.

- **Innovation:** MedCentral will adopt best practices and technologies.

- **Customer Service:** MedCentral will meet or exceed the expectations of patients and families, and address the health care needs of our community.

Values (I CARE):

- **Integrity:** We at MedCentral take pride in upholding the highest standards, both morally and professionally.

- **Compassion:** We recognize the needs of others with patience, generosity and kindness.

- **Accountability:** We accept responsibility for our actions.

- **Respect:**   We acknowledge the rights of others and accept their unique needs and beliefs.

- **Excellence:** We commit to providing every patient with an exceptional health care experience.

*Source: www.medcentral.org

The Bill and Melinda Gates Foundation's Guiding Principles*

The 15 principles here reflect the Gates family's beliefs about the role of philanthropy and the impact they want this foundation to have. The principles guide what we do, why we do it, and how we do it. While many of them are fundamental to the way we operate, we will remain open to amending them as we grow and learn more about our work.

1. This is a family foundation driven by the interests and passions of the Gates family.

2. Philanthropy plays an important but limited role.

3. Science and technology have great potential to improve lives around the world.

4. We are funders and shapers—we rely on others to act and implement.

5. Our focus is clear—and limited—and prioritizes some of the most neglected issues.

6. We identify a specific point of intervention and apply our efforts against a theory of change.

7. We take risks, make big bets, and move with urgency. We are in it for the long haul.

8. We advocate—vigorously but responsibly—in our areas of focus.

9. We must be humble and mindful in our actions and words. We seek and heed the counsel of outside voices.

10. We treat our grantees as valued partners, and we treat the ultimate beneficiaries of our work with respect.

11. Delivering results with the resources we have been given is of the utmost importance—and we seek and share information about those results.

12. We demand ethical behavior of ourselves.

13. We treat each other as valued colleagues.

14. Meeting our mission—to increase opportunity and equity for those most in need—requires great stewardship of the money we have available.

15. We leave room for growth and change.

*Source: www.gatesfoundation.org

City of Essex–Newark's Ten-Year Plan to End Homelessness*

Vision: In ten years, all individuals and families at risk of homelessness in Newark and across Essex County will have access to safe, quality housing that they can afford, with the resources needed to sustain it.

Core Principles (basic policy parameters):

- Building on the strengths of the current system, as well as the dedication and expertise of current providers, we will work together to develop a coordinated housing and services system designed to end homelessness, not manage it. Housing ends homelessness. Therefore, our ultimate goal is for all individuals and families in Newark and across Essex County to have access to permanent (non-time-limited) housing that they can afford, with the supportive services necessary to sustain it, if needed.

- Preventing homelessness is the best and most efficient way to end it. We will increase prevention efforts and resources, to develop a County-wide "early warning" system designed to help individuals and families remain in housing whenever possible. We will actively promote these services to all who may be at risk of homelessness.

- We will end long-term homelessness, and shorten all episodes of homelessness, by moving individuals and families as quickly as possible into appropriate permanent housing, using a Housing First approach.

- We will work with existing emergency shelter and transitional housing programs to create vital Interim Housing capacity, designed to stabilize and assess individuals and families in order to connect them to appropriate permanent housing.

Interim Housing models already exist in Newark and Essex County. Interim Housing is defined as: short-term housing provided for the minimum time needed to access permanent housing, with services focused on immediate and comprehensive needs assessment, resource acquisition (e.g., public benefits), and housing placement. The length of time spent in Interim Housing is determined by the specific needs of the population served and the amount of time needed to access appropriate permanent housing.

- We will ensure that our system has an adequate supply of emergency shelter beds, to respond to unforeseen crises and/or potential interim or permanent housing shortfalls.

- We will create a coordinated entry system for prevention, housing, and support services, to ensure efficient, effective, and accurate provision of resources. Our goal is to eliminate any resource or service barriers that inadvertently extend, exacerbate, and/or contribute to a person's homelessness.

- Whenever possible, we will pursue housing and service strategies that end homelessness and are also cost-effective.

- Collectively, we will hold ourselves accountable for reaching our Ten-Year Plan goals, and our success will be determined by regular assessment of measurable outcomes and benchmarks.

- Performance will be measured on an ongoing basis, and we will shift our strategies, as needed, in order to reach our goals.

*Source: www.ci.newark.nj.us

Did any of these lists appeal to you? We find it interesting to see the differences in the desired culture among similar businesses, and it punctuates how important it is to define a desired culture based on your unique business conditions and aspirations. In addition to selecting the right mission, vision, and values, it is important that the leadership team discusses and agrees about what each element of the desired culture looks like in action. This step is actually more important than agreeing on the list of cultural attributes. The devil is in the details, and a group of ten executives can have widely varying notions of what practicing, role modeling, and managing to the desired culture looks like on a daily, weekly, and monthly basis.

Here is a summary of the steps involved in defining your desired culture. Your organizational culture is the basis from which you produce results, so it is important that the entire leadership team collaborate to define and agree on the elements that are important enough to uphold even when doing so is difficult. Ask your organization development or training department to help facilitate these conversations.

- Prework: Each leadership team member should research the cultures of the brands they most admire or that model some of the characteristics that you believe are important to your organization. Come to the brainstorming session ready to share your findings.

- Brainstorm cultural elements and the structure you think will best serve your organization (values, core principles, and so on) by capturing each leadership team member's thoughts and ideas from the prework.

- Discuss each potential element and get to a smaller, more focused list that everyone on the team agrees is most important to the organization.

- Drill down on each cultural element to describe what it looks like to lead and work consistent with the desired culture.

- In the coming week, share your description with key stakeholders and observe their reactions. Does it inspire? You will know by their reactions if you have landed on a good organizational culture model. To reinforce the "one for all" aspect of this work, ask each leadership team member, not one or few, to share the desired culture with a small number of stakeholders and then report back in a team meeting.

These may seem like a lot of steps, but once you have your first draft, it will be very easy to update as changes in your strategic plan occur. Are you ready for a reality check? Let's move on to an exploration of how to assess your current organizational culture.

"Community is gathering around a fire and listening to someone tell a story."[18]

—Bill Moher

Define the Current Culture

Creating an accurate assessment of your current culture is one of the more difficult steps to realigning organizational culture. We all would like to think that the lofty values on meeting room posters mirror how people feel and work, but this is often not the case. We worked with a group of hospitals to assess the barriers getting in the way of middle management success, and we started by talking with managers about what it was like to work for this hospital group. Their corporate literature listed their core values as

- Excellence
- Customer Care
- Leadership
- Integrity
- Teamwork

After one-on-one and small group discussions with dozens of their managers, we concluded that the values of integrity and customer care were a part of their current culture, but that excellence, leadership, and teamwork were less evident. In fact, we found competition and turf protection was much more prominent than teamwork and that managers and team members with poor teaming skills were tolerated and often promoted because of their valued technical skills. The leadership team was not pleased but not surprised to hear our assessment of their current culture even though they had not previously talked about it as a team.

Leadership teams will need some help—internal or external—to create an accurate assessment of the current culture. Don't email a list of your values and ask people to let you know if any of them are a sham; you won't get helpful answers. Instead, engage managers and frontline employees in conversations that uncover what it is really like to work inside your organization. Talk to people at various positions and performance levels. This is important because your top performers may experience different things than average performers (largely because you likely give better performers more and better attention, trust, and challenge). Use open-ended questions, surveys, small focus groups, and your observations of daily life in the workplace to compile the most accurate picture.

Ask questions that help people feel comfortable about being candid. For example, you can break the ice by asking team members for two things they most enjoy about their work and two things they least enjoy. A simple question like this will feel less threatening than if you were to say, "We want to know in what ways employees are living our values. Take a look at this list of values and tell us which you agree exist and which don't yet exist in our culture." We have also used a method called "Day in the Life" where we ask employees to walk us through a typical day or week at work. What's often most revealing with this method is what they leave out and aspects of the desired culture that they don't experience on a daily basis. For example, is your summer picnic the only time employees experience a sense of community? We also ask about things like the number of hours spent in meetings, the efficacy of these meetings, specific examples of the last time they collaborated with a peer, their perceptions of leadership, and how decisions are made.

Once you have a realistic picture of your current culture, it is time to test whether your managers and team members are ready, willing, and able to change where needed.

Assess Capacity for Change (C4C)

We worked with a president of a small professional services firm, who we will call Ari. Ari was hired to replace a disgraced president and selected because of his reputation as an inspiring change agent. Six months into his new job, Ari was frustrated because he was unable to implement many of the changes he thought were needed to improve business results. Some members of his leadership team and many of their employees were actively resisting the cultural and operational changes that Ari suggested. When we got to know his team, it was clear to us that their current capacity for change was too low to support Ari's vision.

We define the capacity for change as the likelihood that changes would be successful if they were implemented today. This is an important indicator and something you want to know before pulling the trigger on any cultural or operational change initiative. If your managers and team members are not prepped and primed to enable change, they will likely inadvertently hinder success. This was the challenge Ari needed to overcome.

The C4C assessment has four parts that come together and result in an overall readiness evaluation, as shown in Figure 4.2.

Figure 4.2 lists the four questions we ask to determine the organization's (or a subset) capacity for change and the systemic elements you might look at to help improve readiness for change. To determine your organization's capacity for change, you want to understand the following:

- **Are people caught up on current work, and if not, which tasks are running behind schedule?**—All changes take time, and leadership teams almost always underestimate the time needed to implement them successfully.
- **How are people feeling right now?**—Are they stressed? Overwhelmed? Worried? Feeling uncertain can be a catalyst for change if you take this discomfort into account when planning and implementing new initiatives.

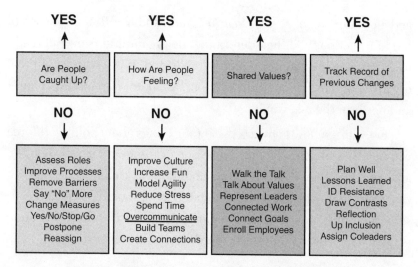

Figure 4.2   Four conditions that affect change readiness

- **Do your managers and frontline employees share your values?**—If not, you want to know where the differences could get in the way of cultural improvements. It is not uncommon, for example, for a leadership team to place a higher value on accountability than frontline employees who might suspect that accountability will give you information that will lead to job reductions. A difference in values does not mean that you should not try to change the culture, but it indicates that you might have some additional work to do to bring managers and team members into the vision such that they adopt it for themselves (enrolling them versus convincing or selling them).

- **What were the previous successes and failures of recent change efforts?**—How have your managers and frontline employees reacted and responded to change initiatives? Have you felt they enabled and facilitated change or made it more difficult? A nimble workforce knows how to make adjustments and welcomes changes as a regular part of the business week.

Based on your assessment of these four dimensions of change readiness, you can create a snapshot evaluation of whether your desired changes will take hold and come to fruition. When we do the C4C assessment, we create a dashboard of highlights and lowlights and an evaluation of *Ready*, *Nearly Ready*, and *Not Ready* for each of the four sections and then determine the organization's overall readiness based on all the information we collected. If you have an internal organization development department, ask them to read this chapter and perform the assessment.

Do you see how knowing these four things about your workforce will help you change the culture? None of the four parts of the C4C assessment will indicate that you should not or cannot proceed with the change, but you and your leadership team should pause and consider modifications to your implementation plans if your organization is rated as *Not Ready* in one or more areas of the assessment.

Create Plan for Cultural Improvement

Once you have defined an ideal organizational culture, defined your current culture, and assessed your workforce's capacity for change, you and your teammates should be ready to put this information together in a detailed and robust plan for cultural improvement. Culture is built over time and one conversation at a time, so it is important to start moving in the right direction as soon as you know where you want the organization to go. DaVita CEO Kent Thiry acknowledged the importance of giving regular attention to the desired state:

> If you care about trying to create a different kind of place, you must start working on it this minute, because if you allow yourself to delay it for any reason you're never going to get there...we'd spend two-thirds of the time on core operating functions...then we would spend the remaining time on how to create a special workplace. If we had put it off it would have been marginalized forever.[19]

We could not agree more! We worked with a client who had a 100-year plan. One hundred years, wow! Can you imagine how hard it is to get an organization to begin supporting changes that would need to occur after their retirement? Most organizations are looking 3–5 years out, not 100 years, but it can still be tough to give time and attention to the culture when faced with seemingly more pressing daily demands. Your culture improvement plan should include the following components:

- A summary and detailed description of the desired culture.
- An honest statement of the current culture and which elements need to change.
- A summary of the C4C assessment results and description of the barriers to culture change, as well as how the leadership team will overcome those barriers (with specifics).
- Description of how the leadership team can best support, model, and collaborate to create desired culture changes. See the final section of this chapter for specific ideas for ways the leadership team can be the change they seek.
- Quarterly goals for the culture change and how you and your peer team will measure success. Leadership teams should review their plan and these measures quarterly or more frequently if needed.

We encourage you and your leadership team to go through the four steps to align and improve your organizational culture together. Revisit each process at least yearly and more frequently as needed to ensure you proactively attend to changes needed to support new business opportunities. If you want to take an initial chunk of time to create your culture change plan, we would recommend the following:

- Plan a two-day offsite meeting, which could be done right after you do your yearly strategic planning (it is helpful to know, even in draft form, a list of your strategies for the next 1–3 years or longer). Ask an internal (organization development or training) or external professional to facilitate. Model the qualities of great meeting conversations and executive teaming that we discussed in Chapters 2 and 3.
- Work with your organization development department to define the current culture and conduct the Capacity for

Change Assessment. Have this work done before your offsite meeting, but do not share the results with leadership team members prior to the meeting.

- Take the first half of the first day to define the desired culture. As prework, share the appropriate section of this chapter and encourage leadership team members to sketch out their thoughts prior to the meeting.

- Ask the organization development department to present the current culture and capacity for change assessment during the afternoon of the first day. After each report, discuss the implications of their findings and have an open conversation about surprises, disappointments, and strengths upon which you can build.

- Spend the morning of the second day creating a culture improvement plan that takes into account the desired culture, current culture, and your organization's capacity for change.

- Take the afternoon of the second day to create a leadership team filter and plan for how you will model the culture. Define your next steps for implementing your culture improvement plan, and add your team agreements to the culture improvement plan.

As we suggested earlier in the chapter, it is helpful to get feedback on your plan. Senior leaders need feedback and don't often get it unless they take the initiative to ask for it. Be open to making changes and revisiting your assumptions and goals.

Are you ready to improve your organizational culture? Leadership teams that model the desired culture will be in the best position to enable positive change. Let's explore what it means to model the desired culture.

"All things are possible once enough human beings realize that everything is at stake."
—Norman Cousins

Be the Culture

While you and your fellow leadership team members do not need to lead using the same style or methods, there are times when consistency is critical. Creating a healthy organizational culture requires the leadership team to lead with one voice; this is the one place where differences may be unhelpful or damaging. As Heinz Australia CEO Widdows stressed, "Ensure your team is supportive, as any diffusion of the message can create a lot of organizational friction."[20]

"Let him that would move the world, first move himself."
—Socrates

Consider that if your current culture assessment uncovered disappointing differences in the ideal versus real culture that these differences are at least in part coming from differences driven down from the leadership team. If you all lead with a consistent voice, the culture will feel consistent at lower levels of the organization, too. If you and your fellow leadership team members are not modeling the desired culture, you will not be able to realign the culture, and you will not achieve your goals.

There are many ways a leadership team can be and support the desired culture, two of which are creating a Leadership Team Filter and using managerial structure to reinforce desired behaviors.

First, create a leadership team filter as tool to help guide your decisions and actions. Once you define your desired culture and culture improvement plan, create a list of considerations that will help you lead consistently with your intentions. Table 4.1 shows a simple example of a leadership team filter.

The leadership team filter is a tool you can use to define what modeling the culture looks like and to remind yourself of your leadership intentions. We created an exercise to help leadership teams fill in their leadership team filter that we call, "Want this? Do that."

TABLE 4.1   Leadership Team Filter (Example)

Desired Cultural Element	How Leaders Build and Model this Element	Our Specific Goals and Challenges Relative to this Cultural Element

The name reminds us that any culture is possible if you identify what you want and then lead consistently with your intentions. Figure 4.3 and the following list show the two parts to the "Want this? Do that" exercise.

Cultural Elements: Select the items that describe your ideal organizational culture.

❑ Feels like a family

❑ Results orientation

❑ Innovation

❑ Proactive continuous improvement

❑ Inclusive – All perspectives are welcome and encouraged

❑ Fun

❑ Learning environment – Everyone grows

❑ Pride in the organization, its products, and its services

❑ Serves the community

❑ People are valued – Respect, trust, openness where possible

❑ Quality

❑ Speed

❑ Nimble to change – Able to quickly adjust and seize opportunities

❑ Service excellence a top priority

❑ Playful

❑ Disciplined

❑ Professional

❑ Collaborative

❑ Informal

❑ Employer of choice

Figure 4.3   Cultural elements checklist

We've used this exercise with several senior leadership teams to help them define their desired culture and then internalize how they can actively reinforce and create their desired culture. Here's how it works.

Step One: Hand out the list of cultural elements (Figure 4.3). As a team, select the elements that are most important to your organization. Although all of these elements might seem desirable, try to get down to a smaller number of that are so important you are willing to discipline, hire, and fire people based on them.

Step Two: For the short list of cultural elements you have selected, discover and discuss the leadership team behaviors that will help reinforce and create your desired culture.

- **Feel like a family**—Be warm, show care, build positive relationships. Be flexible when possible. Remember important days. Celebrate milestones. Share information and include people in decisions when possible.

- **Results orientation**—Share information. Ensure people know how they are doing. Meet your commitments. Be reliable. Measure and report success factors. Talk about setbacks and strategize fixes.

- **Innovation**—Encourage all ideas. Allow some risk taking. Talk about failures as a positive learning experience. Try new ideas. Pilot improvements. Ask for input. Keep up on new trends and methods. Share your ideas.

- **Proactive continuous improvement**—Measure the right things and monitor progress. Talk about processes and methods in huddles. Take the initiative to improve processes. Ask for input and seek ideas for ways to make things run more smoothly. Partner with peers in other departments to improve flow. Celebrate and reinforce even small improvements.

- **Inclusion: All perspectives are welcome and encouraged**—Ask questions. Invite all ideas. Be open to new information. Get your team together periodically to share and discuss work. Be clear with employees about the type of participation and input you seek. Let others influence your thinking.

- **Fun**—Smile. Be light and cheerful. Show your personality and encourage others to do so. Do small things that make the day more enjoyable.

- **Learning environment: Everyone grows**—Encourage learning. Provide cross-training. Model learning. Encourage employees to learn from peers and others. Share information in huddles. Invite people from other areas to speak with your team. Ask questions that draw people into a conversation. Involve team members in problem solving and planning for change.

- **Pride in the organization, its products, and its services**—Show pride and represent your organization well. Share organization news and accomplishments. Celebrate what's right. Participate in organization events and initiatives. Never bad-mouth the organization or its leaders.

- **Serving the community**—Organize volunteer days, work with peers to participate in local professional events and organizations. Encourage community involvement and be flexible when possible.

- **People are valued: Respect, trust, openness where possible**—Be respectful by valuing people for their commitment and contribution. Demonstrate trust by delegating and empowering where possible. Share information and treat people fairly. Be careful not to show favoritism. Don't make negative assumptions about people.

- **Quality**—Talk about quality, define quality, measure quality, and celebrate quality work. Take the initiative to improve quality where possible and encourage team members to bring quality concerns to you. Embrace and encourage audits. Demonstrate high standards for quality.

- **Speed**—Talk about expectations regarding output. Improve processes and remove barriers to effectiveness. Optimize processes to enable people to work quickly and well. Provide training that improves skills.

- **Ability to quickly adjust and seize opportunities**—Talk positively and openly about changes. Plan for changes and communicate the plan and the parts each person needs to play with your team. Do not participate in resistance. Take time to address concerns and answer questions. Work with peers to plan for change.

- **Service excellence a top priority**—Select and promote employees based on their service orientation. Do not tolerate poor service to internal or external customers. Treat your employees as your customers. Measure service performance and communicate results widely. Make decisions based, at least partially, on how well it will serve internal or external customers. Simplify processes—make it easy to do business with your team/department/function. Give internal and external customers as much flexibility and "say" as possible.

- **Playfulness**—Be open to doing fun things at work, especially those that let employees have fun while they get the job done. Spend time with your employees and show them your playful side. Use thinking exercises in meetings that encourage people to play with ideas and topics and help creative thinking. Add more variety into the day when possible.

- **Discipline**—Encourage open discussions about priorities and competing demands. Have the courage to discontinue work that is no longer relevant. Use your time wisely and help your employees to do the same. Do not schedule a meeting unless needed and useful and avoid overusing email lists. Make tough choices when needed and make it a priority to help remove or reduce barriers that get in the way.

- **Professional**—Dress and groom appropriately. Speak with grace and respect at all times. Never gossip about or bad-mouth others. Be open and personable but do not cross the line into getting too personal. Try to keep situations friendly and constructive and be wary of getting into situations that might seem like a conflict of interest (like hiring your employees for outside jobs or inviting some members to dinner while not others). Speak respectfully of the organization and its mission.

- **Collaboration**—Ask for partnership and collaboration. Be willing to give up control and power to invite others to cocreate with you and/or your team. Seek to collaborate on projects and offer your time and attention to peers and others. Develop and use facilitation skills to make meetings more collaborative and open. Reward groups that collaborate, not just individual performance.

- **Informality**—Encourage an informal communications style that is also professional (using first names, for example). Get

employees at all levels of the organization together for communication sharing and relationship building. Use informal communication methods like internal blogs, video casts, and
roundtable discussions. Write information with an informal
tone. Encourage employees to ask questions and to come see
you anytime. Offer informal dress policies when possible and
be as flexible with the work environment as is practical.

- **Employer of choice**—Benchmark what is means to be an
employer of choice and measure and talk about your performance. Seek feedback from employees often and make changes
based on that feedback. Create an environment that optimizes
employee engagement and connection to the organization and
team. Be the manager that employees want to work for
(employees join for the job but often leave because of managers). Seek to develop talent and give employees opportunities to grow and expand.

Now that you see how the exercise works, add any additional cultural elements that are important to your organization and create a
customized version of this exercise for your team. Use the information from this exercise to go back and create a focused leadership
team filter.

The second way leaders and their peer teams can optimize organizational culture is through managerial structure to reinforce
desired behaviors and practices. We briefly talked about your implementation system in Chapter 1, "Executive Team Execution." To
change a culture, you need both leadership modeling and practices
that move leaders and all employees in the right direction. For example, if one of your desired cultural elements is collaboration, you can
improve collaboration by adding it to meeting practices, goal setting,
performance evaluations, training course offerings, informal rewards
systems, and team structures. These are all systemic changes that will
speed your progress and alignment and build collaboration.

Culture is your context for enabling all employees to do their best
work, and it is the key to building long-term success. You can force

employees to do anything for a short period of time, but if you want highly innovative and engaged workers, this needs to become part of the culture. Leadership teams hold the key to unlocking highly effective cultures and can build a strong working environment by defining the desired culture, assessing and improving the current culture, and by modeling the way forward.

Endnotes

1. Bill Strickland, *Make the Impossible Possible: One Man's Crusade to Inspire Others to Dream Bigger and Achieve the Extraordinary*, 137.

2. Peter Widdows, "Changing a Losing Culture," *CEO Forum Group*, May 2004.

3. Kent Thiry, "What a Values-Based Turnaround Looks Like," *Chief Executive*, May/June 2009.

4. Tony Hsieh, "On a Scale of 1 to 10, How Weird Are You?" *The New York Times*, January 9, 2010.

5. Edgar Schein, *Organizational Culture and Leadership*, 6.

6. Geert Hofstede, *Culture's Consequences: Comparing Values, Behaviors, Institutions and Organizations Across Nations*, 21.

7. Meryl Reis Louis, "Organizations as Culture-Bearing Milieux," in *Organizational Symbolism*.

8. Caren Siehl and Joanne Martin, "The Role of Symbolic Management: How Can Managers Effectively Transmit Organizational Culture?" In *Leaders and Managers: International Perspectives on Managerial Behavior and Leadership*, 227–239.

9. Fons Trompenaars, *Riding the Waves of Culture: Understanding Diversity in Global Business*.

10. John Kotter and James Heskett, *Corporate Culture and Performance*, 4.

11. Edgar Schein, 6.

12. Steve McKee, "Don't Neglect Internal Branding," *BusinessWeek*, December 2009.

13. Ibid.

14. Peter Widdows.

15. Edgar Schein, 2.

16. Kent Thiry.

17. Tony Hsieh.

18. In *Words from the Wise: Over 6,000 of the Smartest Things Ever Said*, Rosemarie Jarski, 98.

19. Kent Thiry.

20. Peter Widdows.

5

They Are All Moments of Truth

"Whoever is careless with the truth in small matters cannot be trusted with important matters."
—Albert Einstein

"How you arrive matters."[1]
—David Avrin

In 1987, an important book was written by then SAS (Scandinavian Airlines) President Jan Carlzon called *Moments of Truth*. Businesses around the world connected with Carlzon's ideas, especially the concept that every moment you have with a customer is special and important:

> Last year each of our ten million customers came in contact with approximately five SAS employees, and this contact lasted an average of 15 seconds each time. The SAS is "created" 50 million times a year, 15 seconds at a time. These 50 million "moments of truth" are the moments that ultimately determine whether SAS will succeed or fail as a company. They are the moments when we must prove to our customers that SAS is their best alternative."[2]

We can remember buying *Moments of Truth* in bulk and conducting brown bag discussion sessions to discuss how its concepts could and should change how we view our businesses. We think the idea of moments of truth also applies to how great leaders connect with employees, customers, and other stakeholders. In this chapter, we dive deep into this topic and offer you and your fellow leadership team members several techniques for optimizing your impact on others.

Be Fast or Fail

There is an important difference in how relationships and trust are built at various levels in the organization that will affect leadership team success. Most of the time and for most people, relationships between supervisors and frontline team members build over time. They train and retrain employees, coach them, check in on them daily, see them at team meetings, and build familiarity at informal birthday cake gatherings and in conversations. The same scenario plays out between supervisors and middle managers and to a somewhat lesser degree between middle managers and frontline employees. They get to know and trust each other slowly and naturally. This is how most work relationships are fostered.

It is different, however, for senior leaders. You might see employees only once and for a moment. At a communication briefing. At the stockholders' meeting. Walking through the manufacturing plant. Passing each other in office hallways. Your reputation, which is how people come to know you, is created through these moments of truth, and this means that you need to be able to build credibility, connection, and trust very quickly. Figure 5.1 shows this dynamic.

Relationships with those we work closely are built over time. We see these folks often and get to know them in much the same way that friendships are built in our personal lives. When you communicate with employees only once in a while, they form impressions about you based what they see and hear. You only have an instant (or a few instances) to connect with and be deemed trustworthy by employees, customers, and many stakeholders.

Every day you come in contact with or are observed by dozens of people. You are being closely watched and listened to—even when you walk from your office to the parking lot! Each observation is a

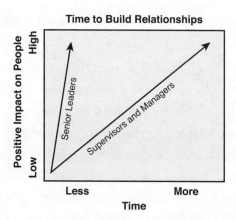

Figure 5.1   **The speed at which senior leaders need to build relationships with employees who they see only on occasion**

valuable moment of truth. Your employees form their opinions about you, the leadership, and the company based on these moments.

Daily moments of truth, then, are each opportunities—precious conversations and micro-conversations. You can use the time you have with and in front of employees to be proactive or responsive. Proactive situations include planned communications meetings. Reactive situations include problem solving, responding to questions, and chance or informal meetings.

Here's a recent and true story about a reactive moment of truth for a plant manager and client of ours involving a burp, a termination, and a sleepless night. We were doing some leadership development work at a manufacturing site. The senior leadership team had established a good reputation with its employees as being open, caring, fair, and trustworthy. On this particular day, the senior team was hosting an important client for a plant tour and meeting. The plant manager was just inside the production side of the plant talking to someone about the details of the tour. Their client was expected to arrive at any moment. At the same time, a production worker, unaware the plant manager was nearby, walked by and let out a loud and long burp. Shocked, horrified, and surprised, the plant manager freaked out and told the employee he was fired and directed him to get out.

For the next several hours, rumors flew around that an employee had been fired for burping. We even heard about it during the training class. In this case, the rumor was true. That night, the plant manager did not sleep well and felt bad about what he had done. He came to work the next morning knowing he needed to respond to the stories that were still circulating throughout the plant. The first moment of truth occurred when the employee burped—the plant manager botched that one. The second moment of truth occurred the next day and had the potential to either improve or wreck his reputation, credibility, and trustworthiness.

The plant manager got his senior team together and shared what had happened, how he felt, and that he wanted to make it right. He called the fired employee to the plant and into a one-on-one meeting. He apologized and offered him his job back. He told him how he felt and that he was wrong to respond in the way he did. He shared how he was on edge because of the client tour to provide some context but not an excuse. The employee accepted his apology and his job back. Immediately after his meeting with the fired employee, the plant manager asked his senior team to hold employee meetings to share what had happened, how the decision was wrong, and how they were going to make it right. They were open and real and dealt with it quickly. This moment of truth built the character and credibility of the plant manager and the entire leadership team.

Every moment of truth has the ability to build or tear down trust and connection. Years' worth of good efforts can be ruined with a single knee-jerk remark or uncensored comment not intended for public consumption. Think about the politicians who have seen their careers tarnished and who have lost campaigns after a nearby microphone picked up a comment they did not intend to share. In our organizations, these faux pas tend to occur in hallway conversations, as people are filing out of meeting rooms, when tensions are high, and when email rants are forwarded, printed, and shared beyond what the sender intended.

Even planned moments of truth can inadvertently wreck your credibility if they do not make people feel comfortable or cared for. One statement, one smile, one handshake, one moment. Leadership team members need to learn how to come across well in record time.

Successful Moments of Truth

You need to quickly create a positive impact with each moment of truth, but what does that mean? What purposes should each verbal, written, or visual communication serve? The most impactful exchanges accomplish one or more of the following goals. The best moments of truth build

- **Trust**—Employees feel that what you say is accurate and well-intended and that you will act with integrity. You come across in a genuine way that gives people confidence and comfort.
- **Credibility**—Your information is trustworthy, and your sources of information are good. You capably share information, although you do not need to be seen as the expert. Your decisions are based on sound judgment, and you explain them well.
- **Familiarity**—Employees get a sense for who you are as a human being including your style, hot buttons, what's important to you, and about your life. If asked, "Tell me about _____ (you)," most employees, and not just those reporting to you, would be able to respond with a few sentences.
- **Connection to you and the leadership team**—Employees feel that they share goals, passions, interests, or values with you and your peers. They feel they have something in common with you. One of the reasons they would hesitate to leave the organization is the people, including the leadership team.
- **Connection to the organization's mission, strategies, and results**—Employees are proud of the organization's mission

and agree with and are willing to support the overall strategic direction. They know and understand results and how their work impacts results.

- **Interest, passion, and enrollment**—Employees sense your dedication and passion for the business, and this bolsters their interest. You share information and stories that add color and depth and bring goals and plans to life.

- **Clarity, commitment, and focus**—The information you share helps clarify short-term and long-term priorities and why the vision will benefit the organization and all employees. You answer questions so that employees can better support major initiatives.

"We are more inclined to follow the lead of a similar individual than a dissimilar one."[3]

—Robert Cialdini

Think back to the last time you interacted with employees—those reporting to you or your peers. How many of these goals did your conversation meet? Think about the last time you walked though the office or plant floor. What do you think employees observed, and what impression did you make? Did you look happy or angry? Energetic or lethargic? Focused or scattered? Did you greet people or fail to notice them? All of these things matter when your reputation is create by just a few moments of truth.

Here is one example from Connie Kocher, an OD leader for a trucking parts manufacturer and colleague of ours, about how her general manager ensures he sets a good tone:

Perry, our General Manager, sets a great example for managers about being visible and approachable. He rarely conducts meetings in his office and almost never calls people into his office. If he has a question or wants to dialogue with someone, he routinely goes to his or her place to have that discussion. He is routinely seen throughout the facility, walking around, stopping to talk to people, and just generally being available if people want to talk to him. His demeanor makes it easy to approach him, and his example destroys any myths about a "pecking order." We try to keep a very flat organization in which anyone can talk to anyone else— regardless of title or position—to get a job done. Perry's example helps establish this culture.

These little efforts make a big difference, and Perry's habits hit on several of the items on our list. It is not our expectation that every message accomplish every one of these goals, but it is important that you accomplish as many as possible and make sure that you hit them all on occasion. And as a leadership team, you should be cognizant of significant differences in how you communicate and build relationships with employees and other stakeholders. The bottom line is that you want all employees to know, have trust in, and want to follow you and the leadership team. Individual differences in style are fine as long as these goals are met and reinforced by all leadership team members.

At the core of each moment of truth is the impression we leave with people and how that makes them feel. This feeling will impact their choices and actions, and their actions will culminate in their success. This is important to remember and goes back to what we wrote in Chapter 2, "The Clash of Titans: Executive Teaming," about how what leaders and leadership teams do reverberates. Each moment of truth creates waves of impressions.

Aside from the opportunity to build relationships, moments of truth offer leaders the chance to go beyond reverberation and make a positive splash. By splash, we mean that people are significantly lifted by the moment, like a pleasant splash of water on a hot summer day. And why not try for that? A good splash can catalyze passion, commitment, and engagement. Some of the elements involved in creating a splash are

- **Surprise**—Are you a pleasant surprise? Do you surprise people or make them smile wide?

Jim's Moment of Truth #1: The Ski Resort

Like senior leaders, consultants need to quickly establish trust. This is particularly the case when conducting employee focus group discussions or interviews. You meet employees for the first time in a white-walled meeting room with the intent of asking them potentially tough and emotionally charged questions. Our goal is to hear the truth, and our success depends on our ability to create an instant connection with people. Here is an example from one of Jim's client projects.

From Jim: One of our clients is a large ski resort with a complex and diverse workforce. They were experiencing some employee relations issues and low morale. I recommended and then conducted several focus group sessions with employees to determine the cause of their apparent dissatisfaction and unrest. A few days before the first focus group session, the organization's general manager told me that I should have a "Plan B" because he was confident that employees would not talk and open up to me.

Prepared for the worst but hopeful, I greeted focus group participants as they filed into the room. I told them, in the most sincere and specific terms that I knew, how my reputation is built based on trust and that I wanted them to feel comfortable with the confidentiality of their feedback. I kicked off the conversation with a few warm-up questions and showed appreciation for all comments. I was pleased when the group shared deep and sensitive information about how they felt about their company, the leaders, and their work.

The first session ran overtime and had to be cut off due to another scheduled session. Later, I ran into the general manager outside his office. He asked, "Have you been in the conference room this entire time? How did it go?" He seemed surprised when I explained that the employees had been very candid. "The dialogue was open and helpful," I said, "we ran out of time."

- **Passion**—Are you showing your passion for the business. Each of us demonstrates passion differently, but it is clear no matter how we do it. Passion fills the air.

- **Fun**—Can you lead and be fun? Yes, and employees will find you refreshing and inspirational when you combine serious work with fun. Work should be fun.

- **Provocative**—Are you making people think and expand how they think about things? Sometimes a splash comes in the form of a paradigm shift.

- **Inspiring**—Do your stories move people? Are you a leader people want to hear and follow? Do your words have the potential to transform people?

We all should make a splash every now and then. Use moments of truth to catalyze energy, engagement, change, and breakthroughs. Go beyond everyday reverberations to shake things up. This applies to individual leaders and the leadership team. Talk about how the team can periodically create a positive splash to reengage and reenergize the organization. We know one senior team that decided they were going to sing for their employees at the end of year communication meeting. They got together several times before the meeting and practiced their singing parts. It was fun, and their performance was highly imperfect. They found, though, that their flawed amateur performance created a wonderful splash and made a very favorable impression on employees. As a bonus, the preparation improved the level and depth of the relationships between leadership team members. Two splashes!

"Your success will be a product of your own enthusiasm and the commitment to that future, and your ability to regenerate the initiative often enough to keep others enthusiastic too."[4]

—Jeffrey and Laurie Ford

Great Leaders Make an Impression

Following is a blog post from one of our favorite executives (writing here as Terry Starbucker). We are not suggesting that every leadership team member start singing to their employees, but we think that the idea of infusing honest and uplifting energy into your communications is a great way to make each moment of truth more catalytic. Enjoy.

Leadership: The Musical[5]

by Terry Starbucker, posted July 5, 2007

Back in college, while I was getting a degree in accounting, I also found a little time to be in the drama club. The club put on a couple of productions per year, and they were always big musicals. I always liked musicals, because I thought it was pretty cool that characters could express themselves by just striking up the band and singing, right in the middle of a conversation. My big moment on stage back then came when I was cast as "Jigger Craigin" in a production of *Carousel*. I got that golden opportunity to suddenly break into song, and I relished it, belting out songs about whaling (!) and about how virtuous men are big problems for women (I was a bad guy).

It was a blast, and I found that I was quite comfortable being in front of a crowd and performing. This would come in handy for me as I advanced in my career to the point I am today, frequently in front of large groups of teammates trying to put into words the company vision. One thing that stuck with me was the uptick in positive energy that always occurred when someone broke into an "up" song—it was like a joy injection. Think of the great movie musicals you've seen—like *Singin' in the Rain*, *Grease*, or more recently, *Moulin Rouge*. (Try watching the "Elephant Love Medley" in that movie and keep from smiling.)

Which led me to this thought—why not use this technique in a leadership position? OK, I don't travel around with an orchestra (or a karaoke machine), so it's a bit impractical to pull off a big production number to exhort a group to give better customer service (although the mental picture of that is intriguing...). However, since I can carry a bit of a tune, I'm not afraid to throw in a few bars of something just to jazz up an occasion. It's one of those off-beat twists that can really create a hook to go with the message, to make it more memorable and ultimately more actionable. My latest example was just the other day—I was noodling about how I was going to 'work in' the concept of "gratitude" as part of a project Ellen Weber was working on, and the musical idea popped into my head. At the end of one of our weekly management group conference calls, where I usually have the floor for a few minutes to summarize our key goals for the week, I mentioned that I was really grateful to the team for meeting a key goal of ours at the end of June, and then suddenly queued up Barry Manilow's "Looks Like We Made It" and sang the first verse and chorus (with some of the words appropriately changed to fit the occasion). I don't think too many of these folks expected me to thank them in quite this way. I got the energy jolt from the teammates in the room with me, and a lot of smiles too. Did it work on the other end of the phone line? I got a few messages afterwards that it did, from people who expressed an appreciation that we could actually work hard and have fun too.

Am I really recommending singing as a way to better leadership? Not the singing itself perhaps, but I would say that the ability to "mix it up" and create these kind of memorable "hooks" to inspire, surprise, and show gratitude go a very, very long way towards establishing the kind of productive work environment that will produce better than good, if not great, results. So, perhaps you should take "Leadership: The Musical" out on the road and into the boardrooms with you. One more piece of advice—make sure the song is in your key.

How to Quickly Make a Positive Impact and Build Relationships

Moments of truth occur many times each day, so how do you and your fellow leadership team members ensure that you capitalize on each opportunity? Let's explore the goals listed earlier in greater depth and review ways we can increase the number of positive moments of truth. By assessing your current and past communication attempts and asking yourself several questions, you can quickly understand the strengths and weaknesses of your approach. Done as a leadership team, you will see whether patterns exist in how well or poorly you and your peers are connecting with employees. The following lists our communication goals and methods that we can use to make a positive impact with each moment of truth.

Trust

You come across in a genuine way that gives people confidence and comfort.

Be yourself and show an interest in others. Be honest and as transparent as possible. Don't dodge difficult questions. Invite questions. Share the "why" for decisions. Be open about setbacks and mistakes. Ask yourself the following questions: Do I come across as genuine? Do I walk my talk? Are my values clear? Do I feel comfortable standing up for them and making tough decisions to stay true to them?

Am I both a leader and a follower? A coach and a learner? Do I keep my promises? Do I humbly apologize when I make mistakes?

Credibility

Your information is trustworthy, and your sources of information are good. You capably share information, although you do not need to be seen as the expert. Your decisions are based on sound judgment, and you explain them well.

Be as open as possible. Share the reasons behind decisions and encourage employees to ask questions. Be wary of responses that sound like they belong on a press release. Do your homework and share background information and research. Negative impressions are often formed when employees make incorrect assumptions about what, why, and when. Provide the right information to reduce bad assumptions.

Familiarity

Employees get a sense for who you are as a human being including your style, hot buttons, what's important to you, and about your life.

Let people get to know you. Share some information about your family, hobbies, preferences, and values. Employees should see you for more than formal communication meetings. If you cannot spend time with employees, write a blog or create informal video messages.

Connection to You and the Team

Employees feel that they share goals, passions, interests, or values with you and your peers. They feel they have something in common with you.

Share your goals, values, and vision for the organization. Communicate your hopes and worries as appropriate. Show your passion for the business and be energized by goals, progress, and great team efforts. Talk with employees about their lives, show in interest in them.

Connection to the Organization

Employees are proud of the organization's mission and agree with and are willing to support the overall strategic direction. They know and understand results and how their work impacts results.

Talk often about the organization's direction and mission and tie this to daily work and current priorities. Make sure that employees know how the organization's mission makes it a better place to work. Have a mission and strategic plan that is worthy of their passion and commitment ("make more money for rich stockholders" won't cut it).

Interest, Passion, and Enrollment

Employees sense your dedication and passion for the business, and this bolsters their interest. You share information and stories that add color and depth and bring goals and plans to life.

Be animated, excited, and willing to show your love of the business. Positively reinforce managers and supervisors who do the same. Talk about what drives you to do your job; let people into your work life through the stories you tell. Actively celebrate successes and show an interest in learning about daily success stories.

Clarity, Commitment, and Focus

The information you share helps clarify short-term and long-term priorities and why the vision will benefit the organization and all employees. You answer questions so that employees can better support major initiatives.

Take the initiative to communicate priorities and engage employees in conversation. Share priorities in several ways and levels of detail so that everyone can understand on what they should focus. Show focus through the decisions you make and by modeling an appropriate sense of urgency.

Make a Splash!

Create a positive impression that moves, engages, or surprises employees.

Do something fun and surprising at least a few times per year. Share information that you find provocative. Ask your OD and marketing departments to help your team improve the impact of your communications.

❀ ❀ ❀

Are you wondering *when* you will have time to connect in these ways? We know that time is scarce, but time spent connecting with employees has a high ROI, likely higher than many things on your mile-long to-do lists. Not every conversation or brief exchange warrants that you take these steps, but we think that if you look over this list of goals, descriptions, and suggestions regularly, you will improve the delivery and impact of your messages. Looking back at the situation with the plant manager who fired a worker for his loud and untimely burp, one reason the second moment of truth was effective and built his trustworthiness and credibility was that he humbly apologized for making a mistake and fixed the problem. He shared his feelings and showed his staff that he was willing to expose himself to embarrassment to get things right.

Lisa's Moment of Truth: Asking the CEO to Spend Millions More

Leaders sometimes need to ask employees, stakeholders, and each other to make difficult changes. These moments of truth rely on the quality of your approach, preparedness, and your credibility. Here is an example.

From Lisa: I had been the head of HR for only three months when I stood in front of the CEO, president, and my fellow senior team members and asked them to make an expensive decision to change our pay practices. The CEO was known as a guy who did not like making decisions that cost him money and was not afraid to bend the rules when he benefited from doing so. I knew that our current procedures were wrong and that it would be hard to defend the way we classified employees if challenged.

Previous HR leaders apparently thought they were doing the right things, but they were wrong. I did my homework, including consulting several attorneys from different firms, and I detailed several if/then financial calculations. Throughout my work and research, I kept my peers in the loop. They understood what I was going to ask them to support, the ramifications of the change, and the risks involved with not changing. The change I was recommending would cost millions of dollars in additional payroll each year and cause major headaches for the operations group.

As the meeting got underway, I shared the data and my recommendations. The CEO pushed back, asked questions, and expressed his concerns about the additional costs and how the changes would impact the operations group. My peers chimed in, expressed their concerns, but then backed me up and recommended we make the changes to the pay practices. After an hour, the decision was final, and the CEO and President agreed that the change should be made. Later, several of my peers came by my office to congratulate me on the decision and expressed their surprise that the CEO agreed.

Looking back at this moment of truth, I benefited from focusing on several of our goals for creating impact. First, the research helped me create credibility with my peers and the CEO and president. This was only the third or fourth time I had presented to the CEO and the first time I had asked him to support an unpopular decision. Although the costs to make the change were high, the costs involved in not changing had the potential to be much higher if sued. By connecting the right but difficult path to the CEO's long-term goals for the organization, I was able to build a stronger case and align with the CEO's interests. Lastly, keeping my peers informed during my research made them my allies, not adversaries, and this is perhaps the most important thing I did.

Should the idea that all moments spent with or in the presence of others are moments of truth change how you and your fellow leadership team members communicate with staff? We believe that it should. You might remember the idea of the emotional bank account that Stephen R. Covey wrote about in his best seller, *The Seven Habits of Highly Effective Leaders*. Covey said that every time we communicate with someone, we either make a deposit or withdrawal from the emotional bank account. Covey used the term "emotional bank account" to refer to the sum of our impressions about each other and the health of our relationships. Each moment of truth redefines your leadership and the reputation of the leadership team—each moment builds it up or tears it down. Covey's idea of the emotional bank account reminds us that every conversation counts. Every hallway passing counts. Every opening of a communication meeting counts. Every email counts.

Do you want to connect more with employees? How much time are you spending with them? The nice thing about moments of truth well spent is that you can make a big difference in a little time. If you set aside an additional five minutes a day to converse with employees, it will go a long way. Whether you MBWA (manage/connect by walking around), eat lunch in the cafeteria, or engage in an informal idea generation conversation, you can efficiently increase visibility. One word of caution about the idea to eat in the cafeteria: Don't sit at the "executives" table, as this reinforces separation, not relationship. We have one client where the senior leaders all sit at one particular table in the lunchroom, which certainly hurts their reputations.

The value of each moment of truth goes beyond building relationships, credibility, and trust. Leaders receive useful information from each moment they spend communicating with employees. They learn how employees feel, they hear important feedback, and they are better able to proactively identify and solve problems.

All for One, One for All

Moments of truth are opportunities. Leadership is a social act, and each conversation offers you the chance to build relationships and strengthen commitment and focus. As a leader, every moment you spend with employees, peers, and stakeholders adds up to define your reputation and impact on others. And your conversations define how employees view the leadership team. As a representative of the leadership team, everything you say and do is as if it is coming from the team, too.

Jim's Moment of Truth #2: The Christ Hospital

Building relationships can sometimes start off a bit shaky. Here's a great example of how we turned a negative initial impression into a big positive.

From Jim: While serving as a member of the executive team at this large, tertiary care hospital, I decided to build "administrative rounds" into my busy schedule. I directly and indirectly lead approximately 3500 employees, physicians, and volunteers. In order to get to know people and to build relationships, I felt that it was critical for me to connect with employees and volunteers at all levels, in all functions, and on all shifts. I had my administrative assistant schedule a few hours each week for me to make rounds. My goal was to visit all departments on all shifts during the course of a year.

I remember one evening when I came to the hospital around 3:00 a.m. I walked down the corridor of a medical/surgical floor and saw hospital personnel gathered at the nursing station. As they saw me approaching, I could read their lips saying, "What in the hell is he doing in here?" It occurred to me that this might have been the first time they had seen a hospital administrator on site during the middle of the night (for a reason other than to address a major problem). The impact of the first moment of truth during the third shift was not too good, and I could tell that I made the employees feel uneasy. I kept at it, however, and the staff learned to appreciate my visits. They went from being leery of me to understanding who I was and that I cared for them and the quality of the work they did for our patients. The response I got from doing administrative rounds taught me that to be an effective leader, I need to connect quickly, be real, and focus on building quality relationships with all my employees.

Leadership teams can proactively use moments of truth to proliferate important messages, establish norms for leaders and managers, and build the culture. When employees see and hear leaders, they form impressions about many things including

- What excellence is and how it will be measured.
- How personable and fun the workplace is.
- The behaviors that are preferred and whether openness is desired.
- The importance or unimportance of the chain of command.
- Whether leaders value and care about employees.
- What leaders are thinking about the company's future.

Using the same goals discussed earlier, the following list can be used as a filter that leadership teams can draw on to improve the efficacy of each moment of truth:

- **Trust**—As a team what do we do to build trust? As individuals, how well do we represent the trustworthiness of the team?
- **Credibility**—Does the team operate in ways that improve or hinder our credibility? Are we as open and transparent as possible, and what tools do we use to increase information sharing?
- **Familiarity**—How are we making sure that employees at all levels get to know all leadership team members? What communication tools and practices could we use to help employees get to know us?
- **Connection to you and the team**—How can we draw connections between the leadership team and other employees? Do we demonstrate connectedness among leadership team members?
- **Connection to the organization**—Is the leadership team communicating the vision and strategic plan in enough detail so that all employees can understand it and know how their work supports the organization's success and future?
- **Interest, passion, and enrollment**—Does the team seem interested in and passionate about their work? If a fly were on the wall during our team meetings, would it conclude we are highly engaged in our work? Do we look and sound like a strong team?
- **Clarity, commitment, and focus**—As a team, do we demonstrate an adequate sense of urgency, and are we united in what we believe are the top priorities? When we communicate with our respective functional teams, do we emphasize the same broad priorities?

- **Make a splash!**—What can we do to inform and entertain? How might we change our communication methods to increase our ability to inspire and provoke? When was the last time we gave our employees a pleasant surprise?

Use these filter questions to ensure that you are not inadvertently communicating different and conflicting impressions during moments of truth. If you are part of a team of ten leaders, you have the opportunity to build confidence and trust more than a million times each year. What one leader does and says affects how other leaders on the team are perceived. This is both a blessing and a burden, and we invite you and your fellow leadership team members to seize opportunities to use moments of truth to strengthen the bonds between employees and leaders.

"Simply put, trust means confidence. The opposite of trust— distrust—is suspicion. When you trust people, you have the confidence in them—in their integrity and in their abilities. When you distrust people, you are suspicious of them—of their integrity, their agenda, their capabilities, or their track record. It's that simple. We have all had experiences that validate the difference between relationships that are built on trust and those that are not. These experiences clearly tell us the difference is not small; it is dramatic."[6]

—Stephen M. R. Covey

Endnotes

1. David Avrin, *It's Not Who You Know—It's Who Knows You!: The Small Business Guide to Raising Your Profits by Raising Your Profile*, 6.

2. Jan Carlzon, *Moments of Truth*, 3.

3. Robert Cialdini, *Influence: Science and Practice*, 120.

4. Jeffrey and Laurie Ford, *The Four Conversations: Daily Communication That Gets Results*, 53.

5. Terry Starbucker, "Leadership: The Musical," July 5, 2007, www.terrystarbucker.com.

6. Stephen M. R. Covey, *The Speed of Trust: The One Thing That Changes Everything*, 5.

6

Getting Better Together

"None of us knows what tomorrow will bring. Each of us has the responsibility to prepare ourselves well."[1]
—Captain Chesley Sullenberger

Airplane pilots require more training as they rise through their hierarchy to fly increasingly larger and more complex planes. They must refresh and upgrade their training every year, too. Recall the news story called the "Miracle on the Hudson" incident when Captain Chesley "Sully" Sullenberger landed a large Airbus A320 in the Hudson River after sustaining engine damage due to a catastrophic collision with a flock of birds at 3200 feet. During the numerous television and newspaper interviews that followed the crash, Captain Sullenberger repeated that he felt prepared to do what he did and that the positive outcome was due to the training that he and his crew had received and utilized on this day. Their training and experience enabled them to use extraordinary judgment. There were just 208 seconds from the time that plane struck the birds to when the plane touched down on the Hudson river. In fact, the NTSB (National Transportation Safety Board) ran a series of tests using fight simulators to see if the captain could have or should have returned to nearby LaGuardia airport instead of landing in the water. When pilots in the simulator began their return immediately after the bird strike, they were able to make it back to the airport. When the pilots in the simulator were delayed by just 30 seconds, all of them crashed short of the airport. Every second mattered, and Sullenberger knew that his options had narrowed to one.

We share this example because the way people think about leadership competence and growth is often very different than how they think about technical skill development. In organizations, leaders often receive less training and guidance as they rise up the corporate ladder. They receive less feedback, too. Many organizations use helpful 360-degree instruments but leave out the senior team. Don't do this! Senior leaders need *more* feedback, not less. And while we hope that all senior leaders have gotten to their positions based on their previous strong leadership performance, they still need to continue learning.

Here's the conundrum. The decisions senior leaders make and the behaviors they model create the organization and impact everything and everyone. And yet these executives tend to receive less feedback and less training than middle managers and frontline supervisors. Some leaders learn from executive coaches, which is a plus and helpful. In addition to using outside coaching, leadership team members can and should benefit from team-based learning and peer mentoring and coaching. In this chapter, we provide a framework for thinking about senior leadership competencies and offer suggestions for how you and your fellow leadership team members can help each other build and use leadership skills.

"I not only use all the brains that I have, but all that I can borrow."
—Woodrow Wilson

This book focuses on how the leadership team can improve its effectiveness, and this model extends well to learning. If you and your team read this book, you should each come away with the list of potential ways the team can learn to get better together. You can use your lists and the ideas presented in this chapter to get started.

Leadership as a Learnable Craft

Here is a provocative blog post from a colleague of ours that emphasizes how leadership is a craft. And it is precisely because it is a craft that we advocate a healthy leadership team approach to continuous learning.

Can Leadership Be Taught?[2]
by Wally Bock, posted October 13, 2009

Lane Wallace's blog at the *Atlantic* just had a post with the title: "Can good leadership be learned?" I think that's probably not the original title because the URL shows "can good leadership be taught." The post has valuable insights and observations. But I'm caught by what I think was the original title. And I think it comes down to what you mean by "taught." You teach subjects like geography one way. You can teach leadership that way, too. Then the person being taught will get a lot of theory and perhaps some history of leadership. That's not bad, but it's not close to teaching leadership. Leadership is not a subject. You can think of it as a way of doing things. So you may think that you can teach it like you teach swimming. You'd be partially right.

You teach swimming by teaching individual moves, then combining them, then putting the student into the pool to try them. Then the student develops skill, hopefully with helpful feedback.

There are parts of leadership that you can teach that way. In class and my Working Supervisor's Support Kit, I teach some of them. I can teach you how to analyze a supervisory situation and how to talk to a team member about performance and how to write good documentation. But leadership is not simply a set of behaviors. You can think of it as a way of viewing the world, making judgments, and making a difference.

Then you have a more complex problem. These parts of leadership can be learned, but they're almost impossible to teach. And it's even harder to teach someone how to do them well. That is why leadership is an apprentice trade. You learn mostly by doing it. You will learn faster if you seek out development opportunities, choose what you do based on what works for the masters, and get lots of feedback that you apply.

Boss's Bottom Line: Leadership is a performance art that you learn while you do it. Seek out mentors and role models to give you ideas of what to do. Read and go to classes to get more ideas. Seek opportunities to develop your skills. Critique your performance. Get feedback. Keep getting better.

Leadership Team Member Capabilities

So what should senior leaders be able to do, and on which topics should they focus their learning? We have explored several leadership team capabilities in this book, and we have researched several other leadership competency lists from well-regarded executive development experts. In this chapter, we bring our ideas about team excellence together with solid approaches to learning. Here are a few interesting examples. In *The Extraordinary Leader*, authors John Zenger and Joseph Folkman cluster leadership competencies based on character, personal capabilities, a focus on results, interpersonal skills, and leading organization change. They then offer a list of specific competencies for each category. This is a fairly straightforward way to think about leadership competencies, and these categories cover a lot of ground. We would add a category called "leadership team excellence" if we were going to follow their approach. What we found most interesting about Zenger and Folkman's approach, however, is their discussion of "fatal flaws." They identified five fatal flaws that tend to derail an executive's career:

- **Failing to learn from mistakes**—"Derailed executives made about the same number of mistakes as those whose careers continued onward and upward, but derailed executives did not use setbacks or failure in an assignment as a learning experience."[3]

- **A lack of interpersonal skills**—"When leaders are abrasive, insensitive, browbeating, cold, arrogant, and bullying, this is a sure pattern that leads to failure in today's world."[4]
- **Not being open to new ideas**—"People feel ignored, their ideas unappreciated and their contribution undervalued."[5]
- **Not being accountable**—"Should they fail to assume that sense of accountability for the entire group, they fail as leaders."[6]
- **A lack of initiative**—"It is the lack of producing results, driven by the fact that the leader does not initiate action."[7]

These and other fatal flaws relate to individual and leadership team behaviors and can wreck your impact and derail your career. Team-based learning and peer coaching are perfect vehicles for reducing fatal flaws. You might be surprised at this statement because career limiting behaviors are so often dealt with behind a secret curtain and kept between the leader with the flaw, his or her boss, the head of HR, and/or an outside executive coach on a mission to fix him or her.

Let's be real here for a moment. Fatal flaws are visible. If you have a derailing factor that is driving people a little nutty or endangering your job, everyone who works with and for you is aware of the problem. Leadership is a social act and is visible. Whatever you do well and whatever you do poorly is known. I think it is highly productive for all members of a leadership team to talk about each other's fatal flaws. (They already know them.) Acknowledging what you already know is the first step to breaking the ice on fatal flaws and will help you engage peer coaching and team learning. By the way, if leadership team members do not know each other's fatal flaws, then you have not developed strong or deep enough relationships! Keep fatal flaws in mind as we continue to explore leadership competencies, as we will come back to them.

"You ain't gonna learn what you don't wanna know."
—Jerry Garcia from "Black Throated Wind"

In her book, *A Conceptual Approach to Strategic Talent Management*, author Deb Tapomoy identifies nine strategic roles of leaders that include navigator, strategist, entrepreneur, mobilizer, talent advocate, captivator, global thinker, change driver, and enterprise guardian. We love the way she defined many important impacts that leaders ought to make. In particular, we were drawn to Tapomoy's definition of a captivator:

> Captivators build upon an established foundation of trust to instill people with feelings of excitement and belonging. Captivators transfer the energy of their message in such a compelling way that people take ownership of the strategy or vision and are empowered to carry it out.[8]

Do you see the parallel between what Tapomoy calls a captivator and the skills we talked about in Chapter 5, "They Are All Moments of Truth"? Both emphasize the importance of how leaders impact others (see Chapter 8, "Leadership Team Strategies for Remaining Union-Free," for more on this). The idea of focusing on outcomes versus competencies is interesting, too, although Tapomoy writes that it is helpful to consider both points of view—and we agree.

A great resource for senior leaders is PDI's (Personnel Decisions International) *Successful Executive's Handbook*. In this guidebook, PDI authors address 21 executive competencies[9]:

- Seasoned judgment
- Visionary thinking
- Financial acumen
- Global perspective
- Shaping strategy
- Driving execution
- Attracting and developing talent
- Empowering others
- Influencing and negotiating
- Leadership versatility
- Building organizational relationships
- Inspiring trust

- Fostering open dialogue
- High-impact delivery
- Drive for stakeholder success
- Entrepreneurial risk taking
- Mature confidence
- Adaptability
- Career and self-direction
- Cross-functional capability
- Industry knowledge

This list of executive competencies is fairly complete, although we would add leadership teaming skills and building organizational culture. And PDI's description of their competency "inspiring trust" is excellent:

Trust operates on multiple levels. To some degree trust is both a character and a competence issue. People want to know if you are honest and open about your agenda and actions, and if they can trust your intentions. They also want to know if you have the skills, resources, time, and wherewithal to deliver on your commitments. Executives not only have to earn personal trust, they also need to set the stage for trust in their organizations. To maximize their organization's value, they must earn the trust of important stakeholders such as employees, customers, and stockholders.[10]

If your organization uses a 360-degree assessment, you can use the surveyed competencies as a starting point for discussions about development. Using a good 360-degree assessment is a good choice, by the way, as long as it is used to facilitate development conversations within the team, not just for the individual (see the sidebar on the following page). There are many excellent executive competency models or lists of important executive skills. Even so, we find that it is common that the following competencies are left out:

- Executive teaming skills
- Building organizational culture

- Building organizational agility
- The executive's role in preventing unionization
- Building relationships at all levels of the organization

So consider adding these to whatever list of competencies you use. If you already have leadership competencies, share this chapter with your OD, HR, or training department and ask them to include skills that help build excellent leadership teams.

Our Strengths and Weaknesses Are Known

This is one of our guiding beliefs, and we invite you to take it on, too. This belief has the power to reduce stress, improve clarity, and make your likeability skyrocket. Really! Our strengths and weaknesses are known. Leadership is a social act. It occurs in conversation. It is visible. And because leadership is visible, what we are great at and what we stink at is known. If we are control freaks, everyone knows this. If we tend to become defensive when people offer alternative ideas, everyone sees this. If we meet our timelines, this is known. If we routinely miss deadlines, people have learned this about us. The ways in which we *add* to the team are known, and the ways in which we *reduce* team effectiveness is known. And we all excel at some things and not at others. We are beautifully flawed leaders—even the best of us!

The reason that adopting this belief—that our strengths and weaknesses are known—is freeing is that this means that there is no downside to being open about our challenges and fatal flaws. Our employees will not respect us less if we acknowledge our strengths and weaknesses. In fact, if we are open and show an interest in reducing derailing factors, peers and employees will respect us more. Your strengths and weaknesses *are* known. Make sure you are not the last to know and that you use the power of this belief to grow while improving your reputation.

More Than Competencies

In addition to executive competencies, consider the value of theories and mindsets for your ongoing learning and development. Here's what we mean by these terms:

- **Theories**—Success requires results. We are big fans of being focused on outcomes. We also know that a good theory can dramatically impact your thinking, actions, and ultimately results. Theories provide context and offer a lens from which to lead. Quality guru Dr. W. Edwards Deming was famous for saying, "Experience alone teaches nothing." Deming believed that behind the most powerful learning was a good theory.

- **Mindsets**—Mindsets are like personal theories, collections of beliefs that we adopt because we think they are right or will serve some purpose. Ironically, it is also common that our mindsets fail to serve our goals, often because the mindset is no longer valid or helpful. (Another word for mindset is *paradigm*.)

Keynote speakers are known for offering theories that shift mindsets. Great books offer theories that can shift mindsets. And executive seminars often focus on providing new and better theories with the goal of changing leader mindsets. This kind of learning feels catalytic. Has the leadership team shared *wow* type learning together? See some of our specific ideas later in this chapter. For now, consider whether an infusion of new theories might help improve the context from which you and your fellow leadership team members work.

Competencies, theories, and mindsets are all excellent vehicles for learning. Determining what to focus on is just the beginning of team-based development practices. Before we get into specific development practices, let's explore more of the why for leadership team learning.

We have already made the case that senior leaders need each other to continuously grow. In other parts of this book we have stressed the importance of role modeling excellence. If we bring these two ideas together, we can see the potential impact of role modeling a learning environment. As thought leader Noel Tichy wrote in *The Art and Practice of Leadership Coaching*:

> It is the job of the leader to build coaching capability into the DNA of the organization. The leader does so by developing his or her own "teachable point of view" and cascading that through the line. When leaders coach leaders around that teachable point of view, learning and teaching are continuously exchanged in a virtuous teaching cycle.[11]

Tichy went on to write that the leader's teachable point of view is a reflection of the ideas, values, and culture that will make the organization successful—the leader's personal theory for business success. Leadership teams need to take on defining their teachable points of view together, coach each other in alignment with these intentions, and then build a learning organization around this.

Catalyzing a Culture of Learning

If you could model and enable a culture of learning, that would be beneficial, right? It will be a win-win when you and your peers do this because you will grow as leaders while helping others develop. There are many factors that shape the culture in terms of how learning is viewed, and you can play a significant role in turning up everyone's focus on building and using new skills. Here are several important indicators of a learning culture:

- People are curious and adventurous. Does the work environment encourage people to be curious and adventurous at work? Does the leadership team encourage curiosity with how it acts and engages others?

- People are allowed and encouraged to experiment. Can people try new ways and approaches? Do you and your peers squelch new thinking and good attempts?

- The work environment is stimulating—sensual. The sights, sounds, smells, and textures are interesting and engaging. What vibe does the leadership team put out in the workplace?

- People at all levels seek and embrace learning in a variety of forms. What level of participation is there in learning events (note: if the problem is the training, this indicator might not be accurate), and how often do you and your peers kick off and/or attend training? Participating in training offers several benefits including building relationships and ensuring that learning is focused on the right topics and skills.

- There is a healthy view of failure and mistakes. People are held accountable, but productive recovery is also rewarded, and mistakes are looked at as learning experiences. How do you and your peers react to failures?

- The workplace is intrinsically rewarding. When people are self-motivated, they seek more learning and development. How do leadership team decisions impact whether extrinsic or intrinsic motivators are more prominent in the workplace?

- The company is proactive about succession. People are developed and promoted. Has the team created a good succession plan, and do you together own the building of bench strength?

- The company embraces omni-modal learning and communication—in-person, over the Web, virtual, formal, informal, one-on-one, group, as part of regular meetings, separate courses, on-site, off-site, and so on. Does the leadership team engage in a variety of learning activities?

How does your current organizational culture stack up based on these indicators? Senior leadership teams have the opportunity to turn up organizational learning by doing their part to build a culture of learning.

There are many ways that you and your peers can support each other's learning. We explore the following four options:

1. Intra-team talent reviews

2. Peer coaching

3. Team assignments

4. Team development events

Intra-Team Talent Reviews

While not all leaderships have this problem, we have found that it is not uncommon for the senior team to be less of an emphasis during talent reviews. We don't mean that potential successors are not selected and discussed; this almost always happens. What can be lacking is a good and thorough discussion of each leadership team member's strengths, weaknesses, career goals, learning opportunities, and potential derailing factors (or fatal flaws). Every leadership team should discuss this at least once each year, facilitated and organized by someone in your HR or OD department. Remember, strengths and weaknesses are known, and there is no downside to having open conversations within the leadership team about individual leadership performance and learning. In fact, there are many plusses including the following:

- When you talk about each person's goals, peers will better understand how they can support each other.
- You will discover and be able to act on common development needs—those shared by several team members.
- Individuals will become more comfortable—more real—with talking about their strengths and weaknesses. Self-awareness is a valuable thing!
- Your efforts will set a good example for managers and supervisors.

Leadership team talent reviews do not need to be complex or take a lot of time. And if you don't want the usual formality of a talent review attached to this activity, you can call it a team learning assessment or plan. The point of this activity is to identify and talk about the strengths and weaknesses that each member of the team brings to the table and to use this information to better support individual and team learning.

"You can't talk your way out of what you've behaved yourself into."

—Stephen R. Covey

How Do You Carry Your Work?

When considering strengths and weaknesses, be sure to assess skills, mindsets, personal theories, and habits. Sometimes *how* we do our work gets in the way or is a unique strength.

Here is a short but wonderful post from senior leader and blogger Dwayne Melancon. We love the idea of how we carry our work as being a teachable skill and something ripe for peer mentoring because we all likely know someone who does this better than we do.

How Do You Carry the Load?[12]

by Dwayne Melancon, posted January 26, 2010

I saw an interesting quote from former Notre Dame football coach Lou Holtz this week that got me thinking: "It's not the load that breaks you down, it's the way you carry it." I think that is very true from a few, important perspectives:

Perception

- Once upon a time, I worked with a product manager who always seemed overwhelmed. He hurried from meeting to meeting, walked a bit hunched over, didn't make much eye contact, and just sounded "down" when you tried to talk with him. His product was doing "OK, but not great" and you could say the same about him. The way he acted did not give me or others in the company the confidence that he was the one to help us drive great success in the market. In short, he didn't seem to be able to carry his load very well.

- In contrast I have worked with people who, even when everything is hitting the fan, come across as "in control" and exhibit a "can do" attitude. They are better able to bring people into their worlds and get them to help create successful outcomes.

- Remember: People want to be part of a winning team's success. Does your team feel like it's winning?

Attitude

- Are you a "glass half empty," "glass half full," or a "you could do with a smaller glass" kind of person? Your outlook and attitude will color your actions, so the better your attitude, the better your results (in my experience).

- To go back to the product manager example, I have also had the pleasure of working with product managers who sought opportunity at every turn—even competitive losses—and managed to drive a successful business against the odds. How? A great attitude, hard work, and a compelling vision. If that's doesn't describe you, maybe you're in the wrong role.

Belief

- Underlying all of this is whether you believe you can succeed or not, which is rooted in whether you believe in yourself. Do you? It's okay to be afraid, but you need to be on your own team—no matter what.

- If you believe in yourself but don't believe in what you're doing, it's time to switch to something you do believe in.

Remember: When you interact with people, you typically either add energy or drain energy during the interaction. Which describes you? What can you do to recognize when you're draining the energy from the room? What can you do to up the level of positive energy you emit?

Peer Coaching

When peers coach each other, they build skills and their relationships. Not everyone is comfortable coaching peers because they feel awkward or don't know how to deliver tougher feedback (like that the performer is doing something unproductive). It is helpful to focus on the present and future goals that each leader has shared and less on reinforcing past failures or disappointments. We love the well-known approach that executive coach Marshall Goldsmith uses called "feed-forward." Feedforward is an alternative to giving feedback that is easier and more helpful. Here is how feedforward works. The performer states how he or she would like to develop or grow in the future. This should be a simple statement such as

- I would like to build stronger collaboration within my departments.
- I would like to become a more effective listener.
- I would like to spend more time building talent.
- I would like to think, act, and lead more strategically.

With a feedforward exercise, each person shares his or her goal and asks for ideas for how they can accomplish it. The "coach" offers a few ideas, and the performer says, "Thank you." Then they switch roles. Here is a description of why feedforward works from Goldsmith's website:

> Feedforward helps people envision and focus on a positive future, not a failed past. Athletes are often trained using feedforward. Racecar drivers are taught to, "Look at the road ahead, not at the wall." Basketball players are taught to envision the ball going in the hoop and to imagine the perfect shot. By giving people ideas on how they can be even more successful, we can increase their chances of achieving this success in the future... Successful people like getting ideas that are aimed at helping them achieve their goals. They tend to resist negative judgment."[13]

We have seen Marshall Goldsmith facilitate 500 leaders doing feedforward at the same time at a leadership conference, and we have used the technique ourselves in groups of many different sizes. It always works because it removes all the mental garbage that often comes with feedback. Anyone can offer you ideas, and it is not so important that the ideas be right, great, or even good. We will all give and receive ideas that are great and ones that are lousy. No matter! The power of feedforward is that we talk ourselves back into our goals each time we articulate them, we get some good ideas, and we turn on our peers' awareness of our goals, increasing the chances they will continue to support us in helpful ways in the future.

"A fool learns from his experience. A wise person learns from the experience of others."
—Otto von Bismarck

We have built on Marshall Goldsmith's idea of feedforward with the following variations that we think are ideal for practicing within a leadership team:

- **Reverse feedforward**—This is done when we proactively offer support based on goals expressed by a peer: "Sally, I know you are working on becoming more strategic; how can I support you in working on this?"

- **Reverse feedforward with a twist**—This is like the previous feedforward alternative, but with a tempting offer: "Sally, I know you are working on becoming more strategic. I happen to play golf with the professor of strategic studies at the University of Cincinnati, and he owes me one. Would you like it if I set up lunch among the three of us? I would love to learn more about strategic thinking, too."

- **Barrier blaster feedforward**—This type of feedforward offer helps to blast away current barriers: "Sally, I am struggling to get my proposal and presentation done and ready for the off-site. I am getting bogged down on _____. What two ideas do you have for me that you think would help me start moving forward again?"

- **Staff meeting feedforward mini-session**—Start each staff meeting with 10 minutes of feedforward. Encourage each leadership team member to ask for ideas that will help him or her have an amazing week/month.

What do you think? Give feedforward a try and keeping using it. This is not something that only works once. If you asked for ideas every day, it would work every day. You do not need to take and act on every idea you get, but you should show thanks for every idea, even the seemingly ridiculous ones.

Feedforward, and the alternate versions we have offered are great ways to increase peer coaching conversations and effectiveness. In addition to *what* you discuss (present and future, not past), it is important to examine *how* you come across to your peers when coaching them. Here is a brief list of behavior guidelines for peer coaching conversations.

When you are the person sharing your goals (the performer):

- Come prepared. Review your goals and reflect on any feedback or feedforward you have received in the past.
- Be honest, but you don't need to be overly critical. Focus on the present and future.
- See peer coaching as help and as a gift. This will help reduce potential feelings of defensiveness.
- Bring courage, honesty, and humility to the conversation. We are all beautifully flawed individuals—even you.
- Don't shoot the messenger; hear the message and consider how it might improve your future performance and success.

When you are the peer coach/listener:

- Focus on listening—really listening, not rehearsing what you will say while trying to listen.
- Forget the past; focus on the future.
- Give feedforward and avoid giving advice.
- Avoid criticism, judgment, analysis, and/or blame.
- No zingers. This is not a good time to make fun of each other, even in jest.
- No comments that produce any kind of guilt.
- Offer encouragement.
- Support action.

Are You Being Coachable?

Coachability is the degree that we are open to what the environment can offer or the extent to which we accept and consider input and ideas. Our success depends on whether we are highly coachable when it counts most. Coachability is a way of behaving, not a characteristic. There are no coachable or uncoachable people, just moments when we are either coachable or uncoachable. Although everyone is coachable some of the time and uncoachable at other times, the most effective professionals will be more coachable overall and, most importantly, during the times when they need to learn from others. When you are being coachable you

- Are not defensive when offered an alternative point of view.
- Welcome ideas and feedback about ways to improve.
- Ask for coaching.
- Reflect on and use ideas that others offer.
- Look for development opportunities, whether in the form of reading, classes, new assignments, or coaching from others.
- Are open to acknowledging strengths and weaknesses.
- Handle failures and setbacks with grace and honesty.
- Demonstrate confidence and ownership for your results.

Imagine what it would be like to work with a team of leaders who all were highly coachable much of the time. Your work would be more exciting, generative, and transformative. It is possible!

Peer coaching is just another term for a developmentally helpful conversation among peers. Keep it light and keep it open. Take the initiative to offer to help, and you will find your efforts reciprocated. Together, leadership team members are in the best position to help each other grow and succeed.

Team Assignments

Each leadership team heads up many projects, initiatives, tasks, and programs. And while some assignments should be made based on functional expertise, also consider development goals when assigning team tasks. Here are a few ideas:

- If building business acumen (beyond your function) is on your list of development goals, volunteer to lead a project that will teach you about another aspect of the business.

- If you have open leadership roles (at your level or one level below or above), offer to oversee and own certain responsibilities held by this role during the interim while a replacement is being recruited.

- Talk about development goals as a consideration when assigning team tasks and project ownership. Make statements like, "Sally, since you want to learn to be more strategic, why don't you be the point person for working with the external consultant and planning our strategic planning retreat?" Or how about, "Sally, you have said you want to build collaboration within your departments, and this project will require that you build a lot of collaboration. How about you serve as co-chair on the project with Jeff, who is probably our best builder of collaboration in the company?"

- When you hold your leadership team talent review, discuss potential projects and assignment that might best serve each individual's development goals. Put the ideas in your plan and reassess as each project or task comes up.

"When approaching challenging assignments in an organization, the leader-coach must be able to evaluate the potential positive and negative impacts of the assignment."[14]
—David Kepler and Frank T. Morgan

Do you get the idea? If you don't take the initiative and plan, as a team, to talk about using project assignments as development opportunities, you will be more likely to assign tasks based on functional expertise, and this might not always serve the team's long-term success. We do a lot of executive coaching and find that there are many great learning activities that can come from being creative when assigning project, task, and initiative leadership and participation.

Team Development Events

In addition to being a source for learning new skills, team events are a great way to increase your exposure to provocative leadership theory and potentially helpful mindsets. We recommend that every leadership team do something in development together every three months. Enlivened minds think better. Better thinking leads to better decisions and actions and, ultimately, better results. In addition, mind-expanding experiences are fun! They remind us why we have dedicated our lives to leading and help us retire beliefs that are no longer serving us, the team, or our organization. When was the last time your leadership team got together to learn? Consider the following ideas:

✓ Invite a speaker to kick off your next planning retreat.

✓ Attend a conference or seminar together.

✓ Read and discuss the latest hot book (be wary of cascading every great book down through your organization as a flavor-of-the-month type thing).

✓ Bring in a brilliant consultant that one of you saw speak.

✓ Attend a Cirque du Soleil (or similar) performance the night before a strategic planning meeting. How might this impact the creativity of the group?

✓ Attend a concert to witness a virtuoso in action (classical music or someone like Tony Bennett). It is certain that seeing a virtuoso will change how you lead.

✓ Ask rising stars within your organization to spend one hour talking about their philosophies and approaches and work influences.

✓ Go on a benchmarking trip together to tour an admired company and take their senior team to lunch and swap stories.

The options are endless, and you should select events that best meet your needs and interests as a team. Here is an example that combines a couple of these ideas.

From Lisa: Earlier in my career, I worked at Mead Paper. I had the opportunity to attend their yearly leadership conference in Dayton, Ohio. They had contracted with Ralph Stayer, CEO of Johnsonville Foods and coauthor of *Flight of the Buffalo: Soaring to Excellence, Learning to Let Employees Lead*, to do the keynote speech and lead breakout discussions. As a member of the HR team, I was asked to help facilitate the break out discussions and got to work closely with Ralph. After his talk, which was amazing, I immediately started thinking about how Ralph could help the senior team back at my plant. A few months later, we brought Ralph in to work with the senior team, and the chemistry was very good. Ralph's messages and coaching was just what the team needed. We ended up working with Ralph for a year and went to his company to tour the sausage-making plant and learn more about how his approach to leadership looks in action and at all levels. What started off as a keynote speech turned into a collaborative development experience and vastly improved the efficacy of the senior leadership team.

You never know what each learning event might bring to your team in terms of improved thinking and team relationships, but the possibilities are endless. Learning events are perhaps the easiest ways you and your peers can help support each other's learning. And they are fun and hold the promise to help reinvigorate your passion for the business.

In this chapter, we shared dozens of ways you and your fellow team members can learn together. We hope you talk about team and individual development periodically and use events, assignments, and coaching conversations to bring out the best in each other.

"Everyone has talent. What is rare is the courage to follow that talent to the dark place where it leads."

—Erica Jong

Endnotes

1. In Aubrey Cohen, "Pilot Sullenberger spins life lessons from Hudson landing," *Seattle PI* blog, March 8, 2010, http://blog.seattlepi.com/aerospace/archives/197075.asp.

2. Wally Bock, "Can Leadership Be Taught?", October 13, 2009, http://blog.threestarleadership.com.

3. John Zenger and Joseph Folkman, *The Extraordinary Leader: Turning Good Managers into Great Leaders*, 155.

4. Ibid, 156.

5. Ibid, 157.

6. Ibid.

7. Ibid.

8. Deb Tapomoy, *A Conceptual Approach to Strategic Talent Management*, 57.

9. Susan Gebelein, et al., *Successful Executive's Handbook*, 253.

10. Ibid.

11. In Howard Morgan, et al., *The Art and Practice of Leadership Coaching: 50 Top Executive Coaches Reveal Their Secrets*, 122.

12. Dwayne Melancon, "How do you carry the load?" January 26, 2010, http://genuinecuriosity.com/genuinecuriosity/2010/1/26/how-do-you-carry-the-load.html.

13. Marshall Goldsmith, "Try Feedforward Instead of Feedback," 2002.

14. In Howard Morgan, et al., 238.

7

Creating an Agile Organization

"No man ever steps in the same river twice, for it's not the same river and he's not the same man."
—Heraclitus

While each leader should build his or her own adaptability, creating Organizational Agility (OA) is the leadership team's work. Why? To become more agile, organizations need to build a culture of nimbleness. The leadership team creates and improves workplace culture. OA starts at the strategic level, with undated and relevant values and business plans. The leadership team establishes and recalibrates the work on which their employees will focus. Additionally, to create an agile workplace, the leadership team needs to model and reinforce ways to lead and work flexibly. If you want your organization to build agility, you and your peers need to be clear and united on how to achieve this.

In this chapter, we first explore what OA is and how to assess whether you workplace is agile. Then we define leadership team practices that can improve adaptability, flexibility, relevance, and results. As you read through this chapter, think about how our examples of agility compare to what you see and how you feel at work.

A Primer on Organizational Agility

Our organizations face unprecedented levels of change and the rate and frequency of changes will likely continue to rise. The models, practices, and tools we have used in the past to enable and manage change (for example, transition management, action research, Kaizen, lean, process improvement efforts) are valuable tools, but they are not enough to help organizations keep pace with internal and external changes. To become agile, organizations will need to make fundamental changes in how they work—their systems, practices, and their culture. Organizational adaptability is created through continual efforts to build nimbleness into systemic elements of the organization.

Another challenge organizations face is how to go from having a change-resistant atmosphere to an agile one. This requires leapfrogging over—or moving quickly through—the intermediate steps of becoming change-tolerant and pro-change, as pictured in Figure 7.1.

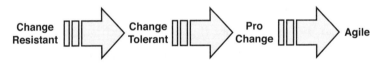

Figure 7.1   Stages involved in moving from being change-resistant to agile

What Is Organizational Agility?

OA is your enterprise's capacity to be consistently adaptable without having to change. It is the efficiency with which your organization can respond to nonstop change. Let's break this definition down a bit:

- What does it mean to be consistently adaptable?
- What does "without having to change" look like? What would this look like in the world of sports or the arts?

- What does the phrase "efficiency with which your organization can respond to nonstop change" mean, and how does this contrast more traditional change management techniques and methods?

When we are consistently adaptable, we can modify how, when, and where something is completed with the same confidence and efficiency that we use to run a routine report. Zigging and zagging is second-nature, and being adaptable does not cause great stress or worry. In their article, "Quarterbacking Real and Rapid Organizational Improvement," authors Longenecker, Papp, and Stansfield, emphasized how important it is to make adjustments:

> It is imperative to make adjustments quickly when things are not working as planned. One of the most important findings about successful leaders of change is the simple fact that they tend to be very timely in making decisions, solving problems, removing roadblocks, and fighting the tyranny of the urgent... In business, the wrong people might be on a project, analysis paralysis might set in, or excessive meeting might cause the effort to stagnate. These types of situations often go unnoticed until the cumulative negative effect takes momentum out of the drive.[1]

Our definition of OA states that we can adjust without having to change. To illustrate what this means and how it looks in action, imagine a top professional golfer named Jack. In between tournaments, Jack practices a couple dozen shots using all the golf clubs in his bag. Each course he plays presents new challenges and potential golf shot scenarios. To ensure he practices some of the tougher but less common shots (for professionals, anyway), Jack puts golf balls in sand traps, in the rough, in front of trees, and in bad lies. He does this to practice hard shots and build his ability to recover from difficult situations. While in a tournament, Jack will need to shoot the ball from new distances and under new conditions. His previous practice sessions, however, will enable him to make many of these shots without having to learn something new or change as a golfer. When leaders, managers, and team members practice a variety of ways to work, they can respond to change without having to change. We learn how to prepare well, contingency plan, transfer, and apply previous similar experiences and act under somewhat ambiguous circumstances.

When individuals resist change, the efficiency with which they can adapt is reduced because part of their attention and time is spent moving away from the direction of progress. When we do not resist and are highly adaptable, we can progress toward our goals faster and with fewer diversions. Resistance creates organizational mental garbage that can build up and become a culture you don't want to combat.

Agility is a systems-based (organizational systems, not IT) capacity, not an individual trait. It takes more than will, or an open mind, to be flexible. An agile organization brings together people, processes, and systems to manifest the organization's mission and strategies. OA is a critical competence for any organization facing nonstop change and increased competition. Agility will allow your organization to build into everyday practices an ability to nimbly respond to changing circumstances and take advantage of emerging opportunities. When your organization is agile, changes do not stress people or the system, as being adaptable is a normal way of working. The level of fluidity and flexibility you and your team need will depend on the quantity and speed of changes to which your organization must respond.

When thinking about agility, it is important to pay attention to the whole system and simultaneously improve the nimbleness of direction, focus, speed, quality, and sustainability. In their article "Building Agility, Resilience and Performance in Turbulent Environments" in *People and Strategy* (a journal produced by the Human Resource Planning Society), authors McCann, Selsky, and Lee emphasized the importance of a systemic approach to building OA:

> We are struck by how the agility and resilience literatures focus on individuals, team, and organizations, but rarely two or more of these at the same time. Emphasizing agility-building

interventions such as systems thinking or creative problem-solving workshops at an individual or team level may be helpful, but if efforts to build agility across the organization are weak, then individual and team-level efforts ultimately fail.[2]

Leadership teams are in a unique position to oversee and ensure systemic changes that improve agility and position the organization for greater success. Agile organizations must have the staying power to drive business performance over the long run *and* the ability to quickly shift its focus across business units and teams. This high level of performance can only be achieved when OA becomes a value and strategic imperative, and this is achieved through a comprehensive tuning of various systemic elements and a consistent modeling from all leaders.

Model of Organizational Agility

Three types of agility are summarized in Figure 7.2. To be optimally adaptable and nimble, you and your leadership team should endeavor to strengthen the agility of each of type and the systems and practices that support them.

Elements of an Agile Organization

Focus (Direction)	Resources (Speed)	Performance (Efficiency)	
Elements: Mission Strategies Goals Business Plans	**Elements:** People Money Capital Outputs Brand Elements	**Elements:** Data Processes Performance Mgt. ROI Measures	Discover Decide Change Measure
Considerations: Risk Assessments SWOT Foresight Value Evaluation Market Trends	**Considerations:** JIT Teams Rapid Reskilling Reallocation Integration Reconfiguration Partnerships	**Considerations:** Process Imp. New ROI Measures Org. Learning Culture Technologies Collaboration	

Figure 7.2　Elements of OA organized in three types of agility: focus, resources, and performance

Focus

The measure of *focus* agility is the degree to which your organization can and does nimbly adjust its mission, strategies and goals (where it is heading) to respond to new threats, opportunities, or business conditions. Agile organizations read their markets (current and potential customers, competitors, trends, regulatory environments, and so on), scan their external and internal environments, understand emerging opportunities, and quickly turn the information into a road map for action. To improve focus agility, your systems and practices need to not only tolerate change, but also be designed to prompt leaders at all levels to regularly recalibrate and adjust the organization's focus. And all employees should be expected, encouraged, and rewarded for keeping their eyes and ears open for helpful information and sharing this business intelligence.

Focus agility is most visible when applied to broad strategies but is also important on the departmental level. Leaders who fail to adjust the direction of their work groups will find it difficult to optimize results and performance.

Resources

Resources agility is achieved through a continual redeployment of people, processes, money, capital, and other organizational assets. To achieve resources agility, leaders need to have systems in place that alert them when a reallocation is warranted and could better serve the organization's mission and strategies. Agile organizations do not leave the potential need for resources reallocations to chance, nor do they tolerate an ad-hoc approach to management. If nonstop change is an organizational reality, then it is important to regularly reassign assets to meet today's and tomorrow's needs.

While it is almost always the case that resources agility should follow a change in focus (mission, strategies, goals), it might also be needed in absence of a change in focus. Agile leaders measure progress and use data to proactively reallocate resources to better achieve goals. It is also common that changes in performance agility impact how resources are allocated and used.

Performance

Of the types of OA, *performance* agility is perhaps the most commonly practiced. Many businesses use efficiency tools and practices such as Lean, Kaizan, quality processes, Theory of Constraints, and Agile (not to be confused with OA) to improve their processes and ways of getting the work done.

In addition to creating agile processes, it is important to create agile people, teams, and cultures. As is the case with operational processes, we need to continually adjust and align how people do their jobs and how people work together. It is not enough to ensure that people are accepting of change; they need to advocate and initiate change.

Work cultures are thought to be slow and difficult to change, which is often the case. Agile organizations, however, have learned how to identify core elements of their desired culture and quickly replace obsolete notions, practices, and beliefs. Agile cultures encourage employees to discuss and challenge (in a culturally acceptable way) business practices, values, operating methods, and work processes as this is an important way that leaders learn the information they need to keep business results on track to achieve goals.

In addition to the three types of agility, our model of OA provides some insight into the systemic elements ("Elements") most involved for each type and the tools and methods ("Considerations") you can use to improve agility. Focus agility, for example, requires a continual evolution and realignment of an organization's mission, strategies, goals and business plans. Goals will need adjustment more frequently than your mission, likely, but all aspects of how you define your organization's path need to be re-evaluated to ensure they represent your current needs and are not inadvertently in conflict with one another. To ensure alignment between these direction setting systems, leadership teams use risk assessments, SWOT analysis (strengths, weaknesses, opportunities, threats), foresight and forecasting, value evaluations, market trending and other methods that help the team make informed decisions about direction.

When it comes to resources agility, the primary systemic elements at play are people (which includes all costs associated with people), money, capital expenditures, outputs (used internally or sold externally), and brand elements. For many organizations, their brand(s) is as much a resource as is their products and services. The methods we use to flexibly adjust and use these resources include teams, rapid reskilling, reallocation, integration, reconfiguration, and partnerships.

Performance agility comes from how well things work as made evident by systemic elements such as data, processes, performance management, return on investment (ROI), and measures. To measure and improve the agility and performance of these systems we use process improvement, measures, learning and development, culture development, technologies, collaboration, and other performance enhancing methods and practices.

Our model of OA can be used as a discussion aid to help leadership teams discover ways they can improve system-wide adaptability and alignment, decide how to optimize these systems, implement meaningful changes, and measure the impact of their efforts.

Five Benefits of Organizational Agility

The benefits of OA might be obvious based on the previous descriptions, but here are five compelling reasons why building agility into your systems and practices is worth the work that the leadership team will need to invest:

1. *Improved competitiveness*—Agile organizations are more competitive and successful because they more quickly see and act on challenges, opportunities, and emerging trends. Their practices and systems enable employees and managers to be more proactive and responsive.

2. *Higher revenues/results*—The purpose of agility is to align your organization to achieve the best possible results. If you ensure your direction is good and clear, your resources are assigned to accomplish the most important work, your processes are efficient, and your culture is supportive of your mission and strategies, you will have aligned your systems to achieve excellent results.

3. *Improved customer satisfaction*—Customers are becoming more demanding, and on the top of their list of desires is their interest in having some say about their experience. Customers want their suppliers to be flexible, responsive, and open to hearing and acting on their ideas. While you might not choose to implement every idea submitted by your customers, if you have the systems and practices that engage them, you will make them feel more valued and connected (just like employees respond to these qualities).

4. *Improved employee satisfaction*—Behavioral scientists have known for decades that intrinsic motivation is linked to how challenged, valued, and relevant employees feel. Agile organizations ensure that their employees' efforts are results-oriented and that their work matters.

5. *Improved operational efficiencies*—If we assume that all change is predictable, then a traditional command and control model of management is adequate. For most organizations, change is not predictable. If this is true for your organization, you will need an adaptable model of management to obtain and sustain efficiencies.

These are just five of the many benefits of becoming a more agile organization. Agility allows for more possibilities in terms of what each organization produces, how it uses its resources, and how people and processes produce results.

Organizational Agility: Two Scenarios

The Food Company

The Situation:

A global food manufacturer company wanted to improve market share and product launch success. Recent introductions of new products underperformed even though the overall market for this type of product was growing. The organization decided that it was trying to produce and sell this new product like it did other products and that this was not an adequate approach. To better align its product development practices with the market, they decided to take on a strategic shift to become consumer-centric.

Their Challenge:

Although the leaders communicated the new strategy of becoming consumer-centric, they did not change how resources were allocated or how work got done. After a year, the senior leadership team was still talking about the strategy, but little had changed within the organization.

Their Approach:

The leadership team agreed that they had only realigned their focus, but not resources and performance. For the following year, they created detailed goals and plans to reallocate resources (changing structure, roles, how budgets were allocated) and to realign several key processes involved in how they managed products and brought them to market.

The Power Tool Manufacturer

The Situation:

A global manufacturer of power tools was suffering from stronger competition, a shift in market (more do-it-yourself stores versus professional contractors), and lower brand loyalty and admiration.

Their Challenge:

The brand name of the tools referred to the founders, but the leaders in charge of marketing felt that a name change could improve sales and market share. They sold the idea to senior executives to create a new line and brand of power tools. To be successful, they needed to launch a comprehensive line of tools in 24 months—much less time than it would have normally taken them to design and launch a line of power tools.

Their Approach:

The leadership team employed all three elements of OA and successfully launched the line of power tools in record time. The strategy worked, and they gained market share over their competitors. To achieve the results, they adjusted strategies, structure roles, the product development process, communication practices, training for cross-functional global product development teams, and their culture. They brought together global product development teams for four days of training (two on culture, teaming, and communication and two days on the product development process) immediately to quickly enable leaders, managers, and employees to adjust and adapt and to play a role in identifying the hundreds of small changes that would need to be made to produce the desired results. In addition, the organization learned how to more flexibly make these types of adjustments to support this and future strategic changes.

Both of these organizations lacked agility but in very different ways, and this is an important point to emphasize. The challenges you face and your system's current capabilities are unique, and you can use the model of OA to quickly diagnose where your team's efforts and energy will yield the best results.

We hope this primer on OA has given you a good idea of what being agile means and how it looks in action. Let's get into more detail now, and explore specific system practices that build the three subtypes of OA: focus, resources, and performance.

Assessment: How Agile Is Your Organization?

We have been talking about OA; it is time now to determine how agile your organization is and where improvements might make the greatest positive difference. This is a systems-based assessment, which means that it will assess each type of agility by looking at several systems including

- Structure
- Short-term Decision Making
- Long-term Decision Making
- Strategic Planning
- Daily/Weekly Planning
- Communication
- Roles
- Education and Skill Building
- Succession Planning
- Project Management
- Process and Task Improvement
- Back Channel Communications
- Measures of Success
- Product or Brand Management
- Human Resources Management
- Goal Setting

Take a few moments to assess your organization's agility using the following worksheet. To get the most from this exercise, have each leadership team member complete the assessment and then have someone compile the results for you so that you can review it as a team. For each element of agility and for each systemic process, determine whether your organization's current level of performance is a "strength" (check column A) or an "area for improvement" (check column B). After you have completed this step, go back and select two priorities for improvement (check column C) for each type of agility (focus, resources, performance). Set two hours aside to discuss the results as a team once the results have been combined.

TABLE 7.1 Organizational Agility Assessment Worksheet

	Column A	Column B	Column C
	This is a current area of strength.	*This is an area for improvement.*	*Improving in this area would make a significant impact on the agility of my organization.*
FOCUS AGILITY: **The degree that your mission, strategies, and goals are highly relevant and flexibly change when warranted.**			
Your leaders have a process they use to create and update the strategic plan on a regular basis (at least quarterly).			
It is common that your top strategies will change throughout the year to take advantage of new opportunities or respond to new challenges.			
Leaders feel comfortable bringing new information up for discussion and making changes to their department's priorities.			
Leaders use scenario planning to envision possible futures.			
Leaders use a methodical but flexible planning process that prompts them to update and change areas of focus on a weekly or monthly basis.			
Goals for individuals and teams are routinely discussed and updated so that employees are clear about the work on which they should focus.			

TABLE 7.1 Organizational Agility Assessment Worksheet

	Column A	Column B	Column C
	This is a current area of strength.	*This is an area for improvement.*	*Improving in this area would make a significant impact on the agility of my organization.*
Your list of projects and key initiatives changes throughout the year as needed. (You don't keep projects alive if they are no longer a good use of resources.)			
Your products and services regularly raise the bar for your competitors.			
Your organization recognizes (and acts on) that changes in other industries can impact your business.			
Your organization routinely monitors competitors and communicates competitive intelligence to all managers and employees.			

RESOURCES AGILITY:

The degree that your resources (people, money, capital, outputs, brand elements) are allocated and reallocated flexibly to produce the best possible results.

Leaders are able to (and actively do) make changes to the organization structure throughout the year as priorities change. Employees perceive reorganizations to be a normal part of business.			
Leaders use an established process for evaluating and improving the alignment of resources allocation to current and near-term priorities.			

TABLE 7.1 Organizational Agility Assessment Worksheet

	Column A	Column B	Column C
	This is a current area of strength.	*This is an area for improvement.*	*Improving in this area would make a significant impact on the agility of my organization.*
Making regular adjustments to resources allocation, including people and financial resources, is an accepted and expected part of your organizational culture.			
Leaders are empowered to shift people and other resources within their department to produce results.			
Daily or weekly planning processes prompt managers to assess and realign how resources are allocated.			
Leaders know how to (and routinely do) change their employees' roles to ensure their work will produce results.			
Assignments for high potential employees are made and changed to maximize their learning and impact to the organization. High potentials are creatively used to fill emerging organizational needs.			
Products or services offered to external customers are routinely adjusted to support customer desires and the organization's needs.			
Products or services offered to internal customers are routinely adjusted to support internal customer requests and the organization's needs.			

TABLE 7.1   Organizational Agility Assessment Worksheet

	Column A	Column B	Column C
	This is a current area of strength.	*This is an area for improvement.*	*Improving in this area would make a significant impact on the agility of my organization.*
Leaders (as a normal course of business) integrate efforts across departments and functions effectively and synchronize them well.			
Employees know how their roles support broader organizational goals and priorities.			
You build in reserves so you can push yourself to the edge and act quickly to respond to opportunities.			

PERFORMANCE AGILITY:

The degree that your people, processes, and programs work efficiently and flexibly change as needed to produce excellent results.

Leaders work together to plan and communicate short-term decisions to improve inter-team productivity.			
Your organization uses a change management process to plan, communicate, and implement changes. Managers have been trained on how to use this process.			
Daily and weekly planning regimens prompt managers to identify and remove barriers to productivity and to continuously improve processes.			
Your organization uses several tools to regularly communicate priorities, challenges, and performance to measurements.			

TABLE 7.1 Organizational Agility Assessment Worksheet

	Column A	Column B	Column C
	This is a current area of strength.	*This is an area for improvement.*	*Improving in this area would make a significant impact on the agility of my organization.*
Your organization uses established development programs to create development plans and provide needed training to employees.			
There is a link between individual development plans and the overall skills gaps addressed in your strategic and departmental plans. (For example, if your company needs to improve adaptability to change, many individual development plans will focus on adaptability.)			
Established project management practices used by project leaders and members are flexible and routinely changed.			
Your organization effectively uses a methodology for improving processes (such as Lean or Agile, and so on).			
Leaders know how to, and do, tap into the back channel of communications (informal communication networks).			
Measures of success are changed, clarified, and communicated often to improve focus and alignment of work. All employees know and understand measures of success.			

TABLE 7.1   Organizational Agility Assessment Worksheet

	Column A	Column B	Column C
	This is a current area of strength.	*This is an area for improvement.*	*Improving in this area would make a significant impact on the agility of my organization.*
You use an established process for managing products/brands and part of the process prompts product/brand managers to regularly change and improve how these programs are managed.			
Your human resources practices and policies change as appropriate to meet the needs of the organization and the employees.			
Your employees seek out knowledge wherever they can find it.			
Breakdowns are openly acknowledged and dealt with. The focus is on learning, not blaming others.			
You assume that you will need to adjust plans and always include contingency planning as part of the process.			
Your IT-based and other measurement tools provide fast and efficient information that allows leaders to be responsive.			
Your leadership team models the desired culture.			
Your organization's ability to adapt is a competitive edge.			
Leaders see training and development as a critical element for success. They show an interest in development and support it.			

This assessment is comprehensive, and even the most agile organizations do not do *everything* listed. Your needs and situations are unique and so too should be your path to agility. That said, if there is one or more category (focus agility, resources agility, or performance agility) of this assessment where you were not able to select the "yes" response for several items, this is likely a great place to look for ways you can improve agility.

How many of these systemic changes should the senior leadership team control or initiate? How should the leadership team proceed with this information? This depends on your organization, but you and your peers should lead the charge to ensure that you and your management team are clear about what being agile means and that you have a clear plan to improve OA. Your assessment and planning process could include the following steps:

- Assess the organization's agility (senior leadership team).
- Assess the organization's agility (management team).
- Review and discuss assessment results. (Senior leadership team reviews both sets of data and then shares with management team and engages in open discussion about points of agreement and disagreement to get to a common understanding.)
- Create a plan of action with the most important ways the organization can become more agile. Include actions for the leadership team, management team, and others.
- Communicate to all employees the goal for improving agility, the assessment results, the plan for improvement, and the parts that the leadership team, management team, and each employee will be asked to play.
- Implement the plan and meet with the management team quarterly to discuss progress, barriers, and impact this is having on the culture and on performance to goals.

This approach quickly addresses the challenge while building relationships with the management team and all employees. Feel free to add and change your process to suit your needs and culture.

Individual and Leadership Team Agility

In the first half of this chapter, we defined OA. Let's now explore agility on an individual basis: how you and your peers adapt and flex. How agile are you? The key to OA is a system approach for using many flexible methods for planning, resourcing, and performance. These practices will be less useful if the leadership team comes across as rigid, change resistant, and inflexible.

Let's remind ourselves of the definition of OA:

> *Organizational Agility* is your enterprise's capacity to be consistently adaptable without having to change. It is the efficiency with which your organization can respond to nonstop change.

Given this definition, how might we describe what agility means for individuals and teams (the performers)? If you are an agile leader, then you are highly adaptable as a matter of regular practice. Realigning actions, recalibrating priorities, and changing your work and how you work are like breathing; you don't even notice it. You zig and zag without causing stress or confusion to yourself or those around you. You don't run around the office as if your hair is on fire when unexpected things happen. And you are more than a change manager— you proactively seek changes that will improve results. Using our Elements of an Agile Organization Model as a starting point, we have created a model for the Habits of Agile Performers (see Figure 7.3).

The same types of agility apply to organizations and individuals: focus, resources, and performance. Instead of elements, this model offers examples of habits that agile professionals use for each type of agility. To improve focus agility, you can use daily and weekly planning, debriefing conversations, reassessments, inside and outside views of the organization, and other methods. Each of these methods improves agility when they become habits, meaning that they are used regularly.

To improve how well we use resources with adaptability, we can practice habits such as one-on-ones, role assessments, adopting a

Habits of Agile Performers

Focus (Direction)	Resources (Speed)	Performance (Efficiency)	
Habits: Daily Planning, Weekly Planning, Debriefings, Reassessments, Look Inside/Outside	**Habits:** One-on-ones, Role Assessments, Consumer's Mindset, ROI Mindset, Yes/No/Stop/Go	**Habits:** Analysis, Share Metrics, Proc. Improvement, MBWA, Remove Barriers	Discover Decide Change Measure
Looks Like: You regularly reassess your focus and prompt peers, employees, and managers to do the same.	**Looks Like:** You adjust and deploy resources flexibly without stressing people out. Your get more from resources.	**Looks Like:** You create an environment where all are involved in making things better, and surfacing and solving problems.	

Figure 7.3 Elements of individual agility organized in three types of agility: focus, resources, and performance

consumer's mindset, thinking in terms of return on investment, and regular yes/no/stop/go discussions. Again, trying these methods once does not make them habit. Individual agility is developed when we practice methods to the point they become habits and a regular part of our managerial regimen.

Improving performance agility will be easier when we regularly use analysis, metrics, process improvement, MBWA (management by walking around), barrier obliteration, and other methods to tune into how the work gets done by your people and processes. Agile leaders create an environment where employees partner to make things work better. This applies to the leadership team's processes, too. You seek to improve how you work together and your work processes (your meetings, your decision making, your planning processes, and so on).

Agile leaders adopt habits that help them spend their time on the most important work and enable them to flexibly lead others. Would your fellow leadership team members describe you as agile? Or do they find you sometimes to be rigid, slow to respond, or too willing to stick with an outdated plan? We asked participants of our leadership team excellence survey to indicate the applicability of the following statements:

- The team is results-oriented and gets things done.
- The team is willing to rethink strategies or ideas that are no longer the right choice.
- The team is willing to take risks after careful consideration of the pros and cons.
- The team looks for and reduces barriers to success.
- The team regularly engages in healthy debate.
- Team members seem nimble and flexible.
- Leadership styles do not clash within the team.

Does your team possess these qualities? Do you see how these practices indicate agility? Figure 7.4 shows how survey participants rated their teams on these statements. Clashing leadership styles consistently rated as common, and this is a concern. When leaders clash, it affects the rest of the organization, particularly the middle management ranks. Refer back to Chapter 2, "The Clash of Titans: Executive Teaming," for specific suggestions to reduce clashing styles.

Let's explore individual and leadership team agility in great detail through another self-assessment that we call the Assessment of Leader and Leadership Team Agility. There are five questions that you should answer about your habits and practices and five that relate to how you would assess your fellow leadership team members.

To use this self-assessment, first answer the questions about your agility. We would also encourage you to ask a few of your peers and employees to answer these questions about you, too. Assign the individual self-assessment as pre-work for a leadership team meeting to discuss agility. Ask your training or organization development department to help you collect and compile the answers to the leadership team questions into a report for discussion at the same meeting. Each individual should first share his or her individual self-assessment before reviewing the results of the team questions. Notice where the

Questions about YOU	Indicate the degree that each statement describes your practices: 5 = describes them to a very high degree 1 = does not describe your practices				
I use a planning tool that helps me and my functional team stay on track. I update this work plan at least weekly.	1	2	3	4	5
I proactively adjust roles and assignments to ensure that people are working on the most relevant and important work.	1	2	3	4	5
My functional and leadership teams would perceive me as open to changing decisions and direction. My initial response is openness, not resistance.	1	2	3	4	5
Removing barriers to productivity is a regular part of my weekly regimen. I do not wait for employees or peers to complain to learn about barriers.	1	2	3	4	5
I assess current performance and needs for realignment in the context of strategic needs and changes that are occurring inside and outside the conversation.	1	2	3	4	5
I embrace hackers (people who go around the system to get things done) and use their actions to improve our systems and processes.	1	2	3	4	5
Questions about YOUR LEADERSHIP TEAM	Indicate the degree that each statement describes your leadership team's practices: 5 = describes them to a very high degree 1 = does not describe your team's practices				
The members of this leadership team are willing to rethink strategies or ideas that are no longer the right choice.	1	2	3	4	5
The members of this leadership team are willing to take risks and think and act big after careful consideration of the pros and cons.	1	2	3	4	5
My fellow leadership team members seem nimble and flexible. They are a pleasure with which to work.	1	2	3	4	5
As a leadership team, we talk about how to align our focus, systems, and practices to produce the best results. We actively make adjustments as warranted.	1	2	3	4	5
As a leadership team, we create a sufficient sense of urgency where and when warranted (at the leadership team level and throughout all levels of the organization).	1	2	3	4	5

Figure 7.4 Assessment of leader and leadership team agility

individual results and team results are in agreement and where they don't add up. Discuss each of the team questions and where you want to score as a team and any actions needed to get there.

If your leadership team is highly self-aware (high emotional intelligence), you can use these assessment questions as a discussion starter about how to improve agility. Used in conjunction with the OA assessment, you and your team will have all the information you need to identify and implement the changes that will improve agility throughout the organization.

As we have asserted in previous chapters, how you come across as a team is just as important, and often more important, than how you are perceived as an individual leader. Agility is much more like culture than it is a strategy or project or task. It becomes a way of working only after honing practices over time. For example, what is the prevailing attitude toward hacks in your organization? Hacks are shortcuts, and hackers go around systems to get things done. While it is sometimes critical to follow rules or regulations, an agile leader and leadership team will have a respect and tolerance for hackers born from a desire to learn about and remove barriers. In the January–February 2010 edition of the *Harvard Business Review*, Bill Jensen and Josh Klein emphasized this point well:

> Hack work, and embrace the others in your midst who care enough to do so. Hackers work around the prescribed ways of doing things to achieve their goals. The benevolent among them do this rule bending for the good of all.[3]

Jensen and Klein suggest that benevolent hacking demonstrates care, and it also shows a sense of urgency and results orientation. Imagine how strange the workplace would feel if some leaders had a healthy regard for hacking while others had total disregard for the practice? If some members of the leadership team are agile while others are not, your employees will not be clear about what's expected, and you will not get their best work. For another example, let's explore the last question on the leadership team assessment: As a leadership team, we create a sufficient sense of urgency where and when warranted (at the leadership team level and throughout all levels of the organization).

Your sense of urgency will determine the speed and efficacy of change. In addition, a sense of urgency helps employees focus, and it encourages proactivity: habits that are crucial to your organization's ability to adapt. In his book, *A Sense of Urgency*, John Kotter wrote about the importance of how a leader demonstrates a sense of urgency:

> ...they behave with true urgency themselves every single day. They do not just say the right words daily, but more importantly, they make their deeds consistent with their words. They do this as visibly as possible, to as many people as possible.[4]

John Kotter has been a long time proponent of leadership team consistency in creating a sense of urgency and in his seminal book, *Leading Change*, went so far as to assert that culture change was impossible if the leadership team does not champion it.[5] Imagine what it would look like if you modeled urgency and your peers did not. Your organization would be thrown into a tizzy of ambiguity and confusion and would become less agile, not more. We have seen this occur in several of our clients' organizations. We remember one specific situation at a high-end travel company. One leader, we will call him Dave, operated with a high degree of urgency. His peers did not share his urgency and clung to the comfort of the status quo. Dave's manager and employees would experience issues working with other departments because they and their peers were operating from different leadership visions. Dave's frustration was palpable, and this made the chasm between his and other departments wider. Had he and his peers agreed on the strategies and projects that deserved a sense of urgency and acted in concert with this agreement, the way managers and employees worked would have changed dramatically.

Creating OA is something that a leadership team can and should do together, and it starts with ensuring that you, as an individual and as a team, practice what you seek in others. Agility enables your organization to respond to new challenges and seize opportunities quickly and well. The work is well worth the effort even if it is never ending, for agility is a continually fleeting state. We like how authors Goldman, Nagel, and Preiss expressed the opportunity and challenge in their book, *Agile Competitors and Virtual Organizations*:

> Agility is dynamic and open-ended. There is no point at which a company or an individual has completed the journey to agility. Being agile demands constant attention to personal and organizational performance, attention to the value of products and services, and attention to the constantly changing contexts of customer opportunities. Agility entails a continual readiness to change, sometimes to change radically, what companies and people do and how they do it. Agile companies and agile people are always ready to learn whatever new things they need to know in order to profit from new opportunities.[6]

When you, your peers, and the organization become more agile, you expand the possibilities you are able to see, understand, and seize. Keep this information about agility in mind as you look back on how you and your fellow leadership team members can and should learn from each other in Chapter 6, "Getting Better Together," as many aspects of individual agility are similar and align with our ideas about coachability.

Barriers to Nimbleness

It would be simple enough to say that inflexible practices are the most common barrier to workplace nimbleness. Here are five types of inflexibility that we see often:

- **Culture**—Some cultures or subcultures enable agility while others hinder it. Does your organizational, geographical, political, or other culture reward slower, deliberate change more than nimbleness? In addition, not thinking about culture or not appreciating important cultural norms can slow or stall your progress.

- **The Past**—We are working with one organization whose difficult history is their greatest barrier to agility and focused forward movement. Although both the employees and management team feel pride that they have overcome their difficulties, the emotional residual still negatively impacts their comfort, mutual respect, and feelings of trust. Have past experiences taught you that sticking with the status quo is safer or more comfortable?

- **Misaligned Intentions**—Do leaders say they want you to be adaptable but then reward the opposite? This barrier is very common and easily fixed with the right information. The first step is to acknowledge what your actions and decisions are reinforcing and make adjustments if this does not match up with your intentions.

- **Time**—Are you so busy that you rarely take time to plan or re-evaluate how resources are allocated? The two most common reasons leaders don't spend enough time planning is their perceived lack of time and that they have not built their planning "muscles." Planning almost always saves time and enables leaders to more quickly respond to changing conditions and emerging opportunities.

- **Bad Definitions**—Another barrier to building nimbleness is that we often lump agility in with change management. When we do this, we focus on events, initiatives, and projects and not on building daily regimens that will improve individual and team agility.

"Haste and rashness are storms and tempests, breaking and wrecking business; but nimbleness is a full, fair wind, blowing it with speed to the heaven."

—Thomas Fuller

Endnotes

1. Longenecker, Papp, and Stansfield, "Quarterbacking Real and Rapid Organizational Improvement," *Leader to Leader Institute*, Winter 2009.

2. McCann, Selsky, and Lee, "Building Agility, Resilience, and Performance in Turbulent Environments," *People and Strategy* (2009), Issue 3.

3. Bill Jensen and Josh Klein, "The HBR List: Breakthrough Ideas for 2010," *Harvard Business Review*, January–February 2010.

4. John Kotter, *A Sense of Urgency*, 58.

5. John Kotter, *Leading Change*.

6. Steven Goldman, Roger Nagel, and Kenneth Preiss, *Agile Competitors and Virtual Organizations: Strategies for Enriching the Customer*, 42.

8

Leadership Team Strategies for Remaining Union-Free

"The moment there is suspicion about a person's motives, everything he does becomes tainted."
—Mahatma Gandhi

We have worked with clients on nearly 300 union campaigns (helping clients win approximately 90% of them) and have conducted hundreds of union vulnerability assessments, and we have seen the same or similar preventable leadership team issues affect organization after organization, regardless of their industry. In this chapter, we share the salient points of what we know about how leadership teams impact how employees feel about their organizations that leads to their seeking or not seeking outside representation from a union. In addition, we offer several focused and specific things that leadership teams can and should do to build a strong employee relations environment—the best ounce of prevention for remaining union-free.

For many organizations, the odds are that if a union attempts to organize your workforce, the union will win. Figure 8.1 shows the average win rates for union campaigns over the last 10 years.

The take-away that we would like you to have from Figure 8.1 is you want to prevent—as much as you can and have the power to—your organization from being involved in a union campaign. Statistically speaking, a union has a better chance of winning an election than an employer does. The leadership team can have a significant impact on the success of building a union-resistant environment. Huge!

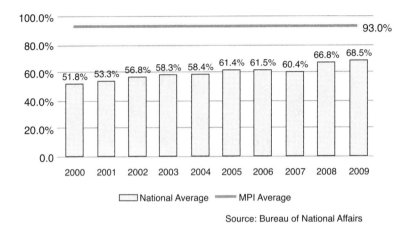

Source: Bureau of National Affairs

Figure 8.1   Average percentage of time that unions win campaigns for representation in the United States from 2000–2009

To set the stage even further on this topic, we share four important lists compiled from our experiences working with clients. These trends and observations feed into the recommendations we share later in the chapter. The lists are

- 10 early warning signs of union organizing activities/interest from employees
- 10 reasons employees organize
- 12 issues targeted by unions
- 12 reasons for union organizing success

10 Early Warning Signs

The following items should become "red flags" if they are observed in your organization. While each item may not directly correlate to union activity, if several of them describe your workplace, you might want to dig a bit deeper to understand what's driving the involved employees. We have found that these items are often overlooked—not seen or noticed by managers—in the course of normal operations.

1. *A change in employee attitudes with a reluctance to deal openly with management*—If managers and supervisors are feeling or noticing a change in their relationship with employees, it may be a result of employees being told by union organizers "to keep your distance" with management. The union may not want management to know that it is attempting to organize employees.

2. *Communication between supervisors and employees breaks down*—If your intuition or gut is telling you that something doesn't feel right (for example, communication with employees), then there may be union activity. If there is a change in the type of issues employees discuss with you, this might also be a read flag.

3. *Certain employees may appear to gain new "informal" roles*—Jim experienced one union-organizing attempt where a maintenance employee started the whole thing. This employee was not well liked or respected, but he seemed to be receiving a lot more attention when he was working in various departments within the organization.

4. *Unusual amounts of attention between different groupings of employees*—One example is where employees may be receiving attention from others outside their department who really don't have any business reasons for interacting with them. You might see different groups of people sharing a table at lunch or chatting in a close circle in the smoking area.

5. *Employees seeking information about the organization*—If employees are asking for copies of such things as benefit descriptions, memorandums, policies, procedures, and so on, it may be information that a union organizer has requested. Use your judgment here, but if a long-term employee is asking for something that seems odd, take note. It could be that something in his life has changed and he wants the information (like a new marriage), or it might be something that the union has asked for.

6. *Seeing unusual groupings of employees before or after work*—Most organizations have a no solicitation/no distribution policy, so employees know that they are not to be talking union during work time. It is important to take note of any changes in habits.

7. *An increase in rumors with a negative tone*—We have not found any organizations that don't have a rumor mill, but it is wise to notice and be cognizant of any uptick in negative gossip or folklore. At one organization, a rumor that the CEO had discriminated against an employee who was pregnant (untrue) started flying around not too long before a petition was filed. Where we find these rumor mills to have a particular negative tone, it says something about how employees feel about working there.

8. *High sensitivity among employees for recent management decisions*—If employees seem to be more critical or sensitive than normal regarding management decisions, it should raise a red flag. Again, this might not mean anything in isolation because we also see this occur when change fatigue sets in. But if you see this type of response and others on the list, it might be cause for concern and will certainly be worth looking into.

9. *Unusual pressure among employees*—When there appears to be more pressure among employees than one would typically expect, it may be a result of "inside organizers" attempting to get employees to support the idea of union representation. Pressure shows up as stress, impatience, worry, and a shorter temper.

10. *Union cards or union material being found*—This is the no brainer. If union cards or union material are found in break rooms, cafeterias, lounges, parking lots, etc., then something is going on! Do not delay your response. It is important to immediately act.

The common denominator or thread in many of these early warning signs relates to communication or the lack of productive communication between employees and supervision. We go into greater depth about how the leadership team should measure and respond to the level of connectedness (or alienation) and the health of workplace dialogue later in the chapter.

Employees in the Parking Lot

On one Thursday afternoon, while returning from a business trip, Jim received a telephone call from a former client who had started a new job as the general manager of a Japanese manufacturing company. While the GM had only been on his job for three days (ironically, it was the three days following Labor Day), he felt there was some employee unrest. He asked Jim if he could come by the plant and meet with him and the president (Japanese assignee) of the company. Jim explained that he was a couple of hours away and should arrive around 3:00 p.m. that day. Upon his arrival at the plant, Jim noticed several small groups of employees in the parking lot. Once inside, he asked the president if employees normally gathered in small groups at shift change. The president remarked that he had never noticed. Jim suggested that he remain that afternoon to interview and meet with second shift supervisors and to stay over to interview and meet with third and first shift supervisors. Following his 24-hour visit, Jim met with the GM and president and explained that he felt that there was concerted union activity and that a National Labor Relations Board (NLRB) petition could be imminent. He left the plant around 4:00 p.m. to return home. At 9:00 a.m. on Monday, he received a call from the company stating that it had received a petition from the NLRB at 4:30 p.m. on Friday—just 30 minutes following his departure. One of the early warning signs was present, but the company never realized it. While the company defeated the union and won the representation election, it had to experience a very costly, intensive, and time-consuming union campaign.

10 Reasons Employees Organize

We've interviewed thousands of employees who have chosen to seek union representation over the years and have found that the most common reasons are the same across industries.

1. ***Poor communication of wages, benefits, employment polices and procedures, work rules, and so on***—When employees have issues with these items, it is often because they have not been well-communicated; that is, employees don't fully understand them. Yes, employees often want *more* pay and benefits, but they also will rally around perceived problems that don't really exist, and this is a preventable shame.

2. ***Keeping troublemakers on the payroll***—Our experience indicates that troublemakers (that is, employees who create problems, have issues, stir the pot, and so on) are often the ones leading the union-organizing attempt. They become the catalysts and the mouthpieces for the entire workforce. They become the reason people start thinking about a union. We are not suggesting that you get rid of any employee who complains, by the way, as this not good management and will cause other problems. But you do need to make sure that your managers are addressing issues and holding people accountable for being productive team members.

3. ***Inconsistency; lack of respect and trust***—If employees feel that there is favoritism and/or inconsistency in the administration of policies and practices, they may seek union representation. Furthermore, if they don't respect or trust management, union representation may be the answer in their minds. We do many employee engagement surveys, and we always look to see how many times the words "favoritism" or "equal" are typed into the write-in comments. If there are a lot, this should be a red flag.

4. ***Not realizing how employees really feel about their workplace***—Our experience tells us that most employers think they

know how employees feel about their workplaces and that fewer actually know. There are many sources of useful information you can and should gather to ensure you know how your people feel (surveys, focus groups, suggestion systems, complaints, questions, observations, and so on).

5. ***Changes in policies, rules, and management not being effectively communicated to employees***—When employees don't understand these changes, they may make incorrect assumptions about what they mean and why they are necessary. This confusion or uneasiness may make them leery of management and that they would benefit from outside, third-party representation.

6. ***Subjective pay practices***—This typically relates to internal equity issues. If there is no formal, objective job evaluation process or system, employees may not feel or understand that they are paid fairly. We have one client where there are seven distinct work groups with seven sets of rules and pay practices at one location and under one roof. Seven! Senior leaders might understand that these groups are different, but when one team is working 20 feet from another team that has a different "deal," it may not make sense to your workers.

7. ***Wages and benefits that are not perceived as competitive in the market***—This objection deals with external equity issues. When the organization's compensation program is not viewed as being competitive with the market, employees may think that a union will get them more money or better benefits. If they are right, by the way, you need to fix this as soon as you can. You will pay, one way or another!

8. ***No effective way for employees to voice complaints or concerns***—Employees need to be able to express concerns in a constructive manner. If there is no formal complaint resolution process, a union may be able to gain support among employees for a grievance procedure commonly found in union

contracts. There are many management shortcomings that employees will forgive, but if they do not feel heard or their supervisor is unresponsive, they will feel you do not care. The union will tell them that they *do* care and will be very responsive to employees during the initial campaign period.

9. *Not listening to employees*—If employees perceive that management doesn't care about their issues or feels that no one is listening, then they may feel that they have no other choice than to bring a union into the organization to speak for them. Nobody wants to feel disregarded or unimportant.

10. *Not following up on employee questions or requests*—Not getting back to people is a common mistake that many busy and well-intended supervisors and managers make. When this happens, management loses its credibility. We have heard employees say over and over again, "If they (management) would only get back to me. And even if the answer is no, at least I know." Employees don't appreciate be left hanging, and this also demonstrates to them that management doesn't care about them.

You don't want to give your employees any of these reasons for seeking and supporting a union. In addition to the ramifications of having to work with a union, these issues indicate bad management practices. Whether your organization is likely to be targeted by a union or not, you don't want your employees feeling disconnected, disregarded, or that you and your managers are disingenuous.

12 Issues Targeted by Unions

Are you starting to notice themes shared among these lists? Based on the information we have collected from union campaign efforts, here are the issues that unions often focus on and around which they promise to improve for employees:

1. *Benefits*—The most common issues about benefits include benefits not competitive with other organizations in the

market, benefits inconsistent within the organization, and failing to protect benefits for employees and retirees.

2. **Communication**—This is a big issue, and the union often presents itself as an objective third party. They share reasons why they think your employees cannot and should not trust management and make promises about how they will represent employees.

3. **Inconsistency with policies and procedures**—Unions often run on a platform that they will eliminate unfair treatment and favoritism. They promise that if employees vote them in, everyone will be treated the same.

4. **Job security**—We have seen unions play into the fears employees have about being laid off or terminated, and they often promise that they will be able to guarantee jobs or protect those with seniority.

5. **Lack of employee input**—Unions promise to represent the needs and wants of employees and that employees will have a greater say and be able to provide more input if they have a union.

6. **Leadership**—Union campaigns can get heated, like political campaigns, and it is not uncommon for the union to disparage the company's leadership. They will tell employees why the leaders cannot and should not be trusted and will present themselves as trustworthy leaders who employees can count on to have their best interests at heart.

7. **Respect/Recognition**—Unions promise to show employees respect and that they will ensure that management respects and recognizes employees. They will appeal to employees who feel marginalized or unnoticed for their hard work.

8. **Scheduling/Hours**—Getting enough hours and opportunities for overtime pay are important issues to many employees, and unions know this. They often promise that the contract will

guarantee them better hours and ensure fair opportunities for overtime work and pay. Sometimes this issue becomes quite complex and goes beyond regular overtime to promises that the union will get employees extra pay for off hours, weekends, holidays, excessive hours, and for particular types of working conditions (like hazard pay for working during a snow storm).

9. *Staffing*—Employees want to know that they will be given opportunities to bid on jobs in other areas, and many want to be able to bump less senior employees if they face a layoff. Unions will often promise to represent employees so they receive more favorable staffing options.

10. *Wages*—Unions nearly always tell employees that they will be able to get them more pay. They might even throw around large numbers, like $5.00 per hour raises and significant contract signing bonuses: "Buy that new truck you have wanted."

11. *Working Conditions*—While more common in heavy industrial markets, it is common for unions to tell employees that they will improve the physical conditions of the workplace or get them better equipment. If yours is an industry with high-risk work, you can expect unions to focus a lot of attention on promising safer work conditions.

12. *Workload*—It is common for unions to suggest that they can ensure management does not increase their expected output and might even suggest that they can ensure that employees will not have to do certain undesirable tasks. They may also say they can guarantee that their work will not be permitted to be outsourced to temporary or salaried staff.

The bottom line is that unions can't actually promise anything except union dues. That will not stop them, however, from campaigning on the issues that they believe will win them the most votes from employees. And although they are supposed to share only factual information, we have seen many unions skew and twist information to increase employee distrust in management.

12 Reasons for Union-Organizing Success

We have reviewed why employees say they vote for a union and the issues that unions target during a campaign. This next list is perhaps the most important one for leadership teams to review and understand as these are the top 12 reasons why union campaigns are successful and why management teams lose their right to directly manage their employees.

1. ***Ineffective leaders***—If you have union activity, and if the union is gaining employee support, you should assume that you have a management problem. Engaged and happy employees rarely support a union. The single largest reason union campaigns are successful is that the management team fails to create a positive employee relations environment.

2. ***Poor communication by employer***—If employees do not have good information on which to base their decision about whether to seek union representation, they might not make a pro-company decision. In addition, it is often a lack of adequate communication, conflicting, or inaccurate information that causes concerns to bubble up in your employees' minds in the first place.

3. ***Poorly trained managers and supervisors***—We have worked with many organizations that either offered very little or the wrong kind of training for supervisors and managers. It is common to promote supervisors from within, and this is a great way to build dedicated talent. But if you don't provide these eager and green supervisors with skills on how to build relationships, manage consistently, and represent the organization well, they may fail. Also it is very difficult to go from coworker

to boss, and many organizations fail to help supervisors make this transition in ways that build the confidence and comfort that employees have in management. We also see fragmentation between layers of management and leadership and a lack of training that ties the management team together.

4. *Better trained union organizers*—Union organizers often have very strong relationship building skills and are able to build rapport with your employees more quickly and effectively than do your supervisors and managers. Employees might find that they would rather work with the union organizers than their supervisors.

5. *More union money spent on organizing*—Union campaigns, like political campaigns, benefit from investments used for events, printed materials, field personnel, and advertisements or promotions. Big colorful banners and all-expense-paid BBQ rallies can be appealing to employees.

6. *Internal/external equity issues with pay*—When employees feel that they are not getting a fair deal relative to others (whether it is true or not), they are more likely to become distrusting of management. They want what they feel they deserve, and the union will likely tell employees that they can make management pay people fairly and consistently.

7. *Benefit issues, especially health insurance and retirement plans*—Health insurance coverage levels is a strong lightening rod issue that plays into people's fears about having to pay huge sums of money if they get sick or hurt. Fear is a powerful motivator, and so if your employees do not feel they are being given adequate coverage, or if they are angry because you recently reduced their coverage, they might be more inclined to vote for a union. The same is true for the amount of retirement benefits.

8. *Non-engaged, invisible management*—Employees will form several affiliations, and you want one of these to be with their teams and with management. If management is neither visible,

accessible, not seemingly engaged with the team and department, employees will form their own groups and affiliations. A lack of connection with management is a significant issue with most of the organizations we work with who have been petitioned by unions. The leadership team sets the tone (with their actions and decisions) for whether employees will feel they know, trust, and have something in common with their supervisors, managers, and leaders.

9. ***Poorly drafted and inconsistently applied policies and procedures***—You want your policies and procedures to be clear and written in plain English. The issues we have seen go from one extreme to another. Some organizations don't have helpful manuals at all. Others have policy manuals that look like 12 lawyers wrote them and that no one can decipher. Neither will give comfort to employees who are seeking clarity about rules and expectations.

10. ***NLRB elections being expedited***—Today, we find that the National Labor Relations Board (NLRB) has a mandate to schedule and hold secret ballot elections within 42 days of the filing of a petition. While a union may have been spending months in its attempt to organize employees (perhaps even without the employer's knowledge), an employer is only given a few weeks to communicate with its employees and to see that they receive factual information to make an informed choice on the union issue.

11. ***Large, untapped targets***—Unions have struggled to maintain their membership in a number of industries such as automotive and steel. For example, the United Auto Workers (UAW) have lost over one million members since its peak membership in 1979 with approximately 1.5 million members. Today, UAW membership is less than 500,000. Because union membership has been on a free fall, particularly in manufacturing, they have targeted other large, untapped industries such a health care.

12. ***Companies blindsided by union campaigns because they did not expect to be a target***—Unions are expanding the their reach and campaign efforts, and more nontraditional markets are being targeted. These employers are often less prepared to quickly notice red flags or respond to early warning signs. For example, health care has become a prime organizing target.

If you quickly evaluated your organization on these 12 items, how would you do? Are you more vulnerable than you would like? Most of the organizations we work with operate under a higher risk of being organized than their leadership team realizes. We would like this not to be the case for you and your peer team.

These four lists offer a succinct picture of why organizations attract attention from and lose elections to unions. More importantly, they highlight the common ways that organizations fail their employees. Your goal, again, is to prevent campaigns from happening or gaining any kind of ground. What impact can and should the leadership team have? The answer, of course, is that leadership teams can do several things to help prevent overtures from union organizers becoming full-blown campaigns. Here are the four ways we recommend every leadership team act to build a positive employee relations environment:

1. Be visible and known and build relationships at all levels.
2. Measure and improve your organization's connectivity index.
3. Ensure role clarity for management positions.
4. Shore up management fundamentals from top to bottom.

"Listening is a magnetic and strange thing, a creative force. The friends who listen to us are the ones we move toward. When we are listened to, it creates us, makes us unfold and expand."

—Dr. Karl Augustus Menninger

Be Visible and Known and Build Relationships at All Levels

This is the most important and easiest of the four goals to accomplish. When frontline employees do not know their leaders and don't have a sense for the type of people they are, they don't feel connected to the organization. When disconnections like these are also found between employees and middle management and/or frontline supervision, the problem is worse. It is also critical that communication flows freely up and down the leadership ranks and that all leaders similarly describe and model key issues, priorities, and organizational values.

While the relationships between supervisors and frontline employees need to be deeper, it is a mistake to assume that your supervisors and managers are the keepers and owners of relationships with frontline employees. You want your employees to be able to say that they see you, hear you, know you, and trust you. Even leaders from large organizations with divisions throughout the world should be known by their employees. Use video, use email, use podcasts, use newsletters, write a blog, and periodically visit each site.

On our Senior Leadership Team Survey, we asked respondents to respond to the following multiple-choice statement, "Select the statement that best characterizes how your organization views your leadership team." The response choices were

A. This leadership team is known by and enjoys a positive reputation at all levels of the organization.

B. This leadership team is most visible to the middle management ranks. We rarely communicate with supervisors and frontline employees.

C. Our organization cascades communication, so only the next level or two below us will feel like they know us.

How would you answer this question? We were pleased that 66% of our survey respondents selected answer A, 19% selected B, and 15% selected C.

You want to be able to select A. Trust us on this. Here's a specific and fresh example. At the time of the writing of this book, we were in the middle of helping a client with a union campaign. Our campaign strategies were hampered by the fact that many members of the leadership team were of little value for communicating to employees. They had not developed relationships with employees, and it would have been a mistake to put them in front of a group of employees who did not know them and had not developed a trust for how they lead and their intent. To win a union campaign, the senior leaders need to come across as open, sincere, and competent, but if you wait until you have a campaign to get to know your employees, you are too late. Our client, coincidentally, had taken our Senior Leadership Team Survey the month before they received the union petition. How did they answer this survey question? Figure 8.2 shows their results.

Select the statement that best characterizes how your organization views your leadership team.

Figure 8.2   How one leadership team believes they are known within their organization

Out of their nine senior leadership team members, only two felt they were known by and had a positive reputation at all levels of the organization. We are not suggesting a direct cause and effect relationship for every leadership team, but we know that in this case, their lack of being known and trusted at all levels had a negative impact on their employee relations environment and on their ability to defend their management team during the union campaign.

And what were the results of this union campaign? The leadership team thought they were going to win the vote. We weren't convinced and knew it was a horse race. The employer lost by one vote, and now their other locations are more likely to be targets, too. The loss was a huge wake-up call for the leadership team, and they are now fully engaged and interested in participating in helping all of their locations build better work environments. And they better understand their role in the company's overall vulnerability to being organized by unions.

To ensure that you have the information needed to understand and respond to issues before they grow large, you need to have communication systems and practices in place that facilitate this valuable learning. To be clear, we are not advocating that senior leaders spend a lot of time with employees—they don't have time for this. Leadership teams need to ensure they create a positive reputation and that employees do see and get to know them. In Figure 8.3 we have sketched out a realistic depiction for the depths and type of relationships you should build with employees at each level of the organization.

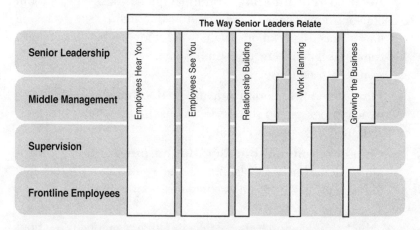

Figure 8.3   How leaders should build relationships, with varying depth by level of organization and time spent by level

Let's breakdown the vertical boxes found in Figure 8.3. The wider the box, the more time and exposure is recommended. For example, the boxes labeled "Employees Hear You," and "Employees See You" are equally wide for all levels of the organization (senior leadership, middle management, supervision, and frontline employees). The leadership team—as a team and as individuals—needs to be seen and heard by employees at all levels. The larger your organization, the more you might need to consider communication tools like videos, blogs, and emails to help reach employees. We do not expect that you will spend as much time planning with supervision; you will spend more time planning with middle managers and with fellow senior leaders. To ensure that the entire management team is seen as trustworthy and responsive, relationship building between managerial layers is critical. That said, leadership teams should spend more time with their peers and middle managers. So what's the right balance? Here are a few examples of what we mean by each practice listed on Figure 8.3:

- **Employees see you**—Speeches, general communications, pictures, videos, periodic site visits, walking around the office.
- **Employees hear you**—Podcasts, articles, blog posts, emails, bulletin boards, employee newsletters.
- **Relationship building**—Informal gatherings, lunch room conversations, copy room greetings, walkthroughs, shaking hands and asking about their work, round table discussions, training sessions. (Yes, we think senior leaders ought to occasionally attend these.)
- **Planning and communicating decisions**—Meetings to review progress and discuss decisions, brainstorming sessions, staff meetings, project updates.
- **Collaboration and building the business**—Strategic planning, departmental planning, idea generation, attending industry events, decision making, post-mortems.

We think this diagram is useful in generating team dialogue about what you are or are not doing to connect with each level of the organization. We realize that every organization has different structures and numbers of layers, but you can get the idea from Figure 8.3. Connect on some level with everyone and then more deeply with your peers and middle managers. We explored many specific ways leaders can quickly and effectively build relationships in Chapter 5, "They Are All Moments of Truth."

"Leadership is solving problems. The day soldiers stop bringing you their problems is the day you have stopped leading them. They have either lost confidence that you can help or concluded you do not care. Either case is a failure of leadership."[1]
—Colin Powell

Measure and Improve Your Organization's Connectivity Index

We created the concept for the connectivity index as a way assessing how connected or how alienated employees feel at work. This is a useful and important thing to know because if your employees are feeling alienated, your vulnerability to unionization is much higher. In addition, high connectivity will improve employee engagement, productivity, and focus. Take a look at Figure 8.4.

Connectivity vs. Alienation

Disconnected from You, Forming Other Affiliations	Somewhat Connected, Somewhat Engaged	Connected, Affiliated with Mgt, Engaged
Less		**More**
	Connectivity	

Treated well and equally, openness, communication, value diversity, I make a difference, fairness, consistency, truth, appreciated, enjoy, likeability, cares, accountability, visible.

Figure 8.4   How employees move from feeling disconnected to being connected, and the behavioral practices management should use to create a connected workplace

The top part of Figure 8.4 is straightforward. As your assessment moves to the right, connectivity is higher, and alienation is lower. And the more connected employees are, the stronger the affiliations they will have with management (along with other affiliations). When employees feel alienated, their other affiliations are more prominent and important. The terms at the bottom of the figure are things we look at to assess connectivity and alienation. Some of these terms might not strike you as obvious indicators of connectivity, so let's go over them individually:

- **Treated well and equally**—Employees will draw conclusions about how you feel about them and whether they are important to you by how you treat them and how that treatment compares to how they see you treat others. Employees will not engage with the management team if they feel you are not giving them the regard they deserve.

- **Openness**—Best friends tell each other secrets. Perfect strangers keep information to themselves. Healthy workplace relationships should be somewhere in the middle. They are authentic—always honest whenever sharing information is possible and practical. Employees will draw themselves in if they feel they understand what's going on.

- **Communication**—The more you communicate with employees, the better. When we engage in conversations about the business, we feel more connected to it. Improving communication is one of the easiest ways managers can connect with employees. We connect with what we know.

- **Value diversity**—Employees will appreciate it if they see management making every effort to treat all people well and equally and will take special note if it seems obvious to them that you truly value diversity. "Truly value" means going beyond a paragraph in your employee handbook to the efforts you make (or don't) to engage everyone regardless of age, race ethnicity, gender, tenure, sexual orientation, or other classification.

- **I make a difference**—When employees feel their work makes a difference, they feel like an important part of the organization. If they feel their work is not valued, they will feel used and like the ugly stepchild, which leads to alienation.

- **Fairness**—It is not always easy to do everything in ways that employees will perceive as fair, but when you do, they will know and appreciate that you are trying to do the right things right.

- **Consistency**—Consistency is a type of fairness, although many managers and leaders don't realize this. When managers lead differently, it can lead to feelings of loss, unfairness, and discomfort. You don't want your employees thinking that job satisfaction depends on which manager a person has the luck (or lack of luck) to report to.

- **Truth**—When you tell the truth, it expresses care. When employees believe you don't always tell the truth, they will become alienated because you cannot be trusted and therefore might not have their best interests at heart.

- **Appreciated**—Appreciation is an expression of value and care, and employees will feel more connected when you show appreciation.

- **Enjoy**—Employees are drawn into, connect with, and engage more in activities they enjoy with managers who they enjoy working with.

- **Likeability**—Likeability may not seem like an important indicator of connection, but it is. Employees seek to be with and will work harder for managers they like.

- **Cares**—When you demonstrate care, you give something of yourself to your employees, and they will be more likely to reciprocate. If employees don't think you care, they will withdraw. And be mindful of the little things you do. Avoiding eye contact in the parking lot or failing to say hello in the hallway can give employees a cold feeling.

- **Accountability**—This might seem like the least obvious item on this list, but we have found that when managers do not hold people who are not being accountable, your employees lose faith in you and your intentions. Failing to hold slackers accountable is one of the most common complaints we hear from employees, and they often interpret this as a type of unfairness and inconsistency.

- **Visible**—Employees will not connect with managers and leaders they have never seen or heard from. When you are visible, you help employees get comfortable with you.

As a leadership team, you need to know if your employees are connected or alienated so that you can make adjustments to the workplace culture, management practices, and perhaps the management team if needed. How can you measure your connectivity index? The simplest way is to ensure that your employee engagement survey assesses the above-mentioned items. We have started calculating the connectivity index with many of our survey projects and have found that it adds a lot of depth to the feedback the leadership team receives.

Well-led Affiliations or Tribes

In 2008, bestselling author Seth Godin published a book called *Tribes: We Need You to Lead Us* that explored the nature of how and why people join and follow groups. We think several of the ideas behind *Tribes* can be helpful to leadership teams who want to build stronger connections with their managers and employees. The two characteristics of a tribe are that it joins people who have a common interest and gives them a way to connect and communicate. Tribes need to be lead and are at the heart of organizational movements. Why, then, do so many leaders fail to lead, engage, or build their tribes? Sometimes it is because we are focused on the enterprise as a thing, and Godin cautions us against embracing the factory instead of the tribe.

If you want to create a movement, which all leadership teams should want to do, you need to make it easy for the tribe to communicate with leaders and to communicate between members. And as leaders, we need to realize that money is not the point of a movement. We have one client that suffers from disengaged employees, and one reason for this is that they are not creating a common interest that is compelling enough—they talk only about money and profits, which are important but not enough. Your employees will be members of many tribes and hopefully yours. If not, it will be hard for you to influence and focus their commitment.

"People yearn for change, they relish being a part of a movement, and they talk about things that are remarkable, not boring."[2]
—Seth Godin

Ensure Role Clarity for Management Positions

There are two problems related to role clarity that diminish relationships between employees and the management team. First, when the roles of executives, middle managers, frontline supervisors, and leads are not defined effectively, the management team will underperform and may appear to be at odds with each other. Poorly defined roles can cause

- Duplication or overlapping of effort
- Gaps in ownership
- Conflicts caused by confusion or ambiguity
- Blurred or scattered focus
- Inflexibility
- Perceptions that management is incompetent

We have worked with several clients who had not revisited their job descriptions in many years and whose management roles are no longer set up for success. In particular, it is common for middle management roles to be too broad and bogged down with administration. For managers to build relationships, coach, connect, and lead vibrant teams, their jobs need to emphasize these skills in terms of time and measures of success.

We have also seen a lot of role fuzziness at the frontline supervisor level. When these individuals aren't sure if they are management or don't know how being management ought to change how they work, well-intended communication, goals, and standards that come from senior leadership teams and middle management may stall or be poorly implemented.

The second problem with poorly designed management roles is the tension that it causes between leaders, managers, and supervisors. This is a serious challenge because it can wreck your efforts to build a strong culture and build organizational agility. You could define a desired culture, do a wonderful job communicating your intentions, and then fail to produce positive cultural change because you and your management team are not on the same page about things.

As a leadership team, you want to make sure that your management team is set up for success and ready to turn strategies and goals into results while engaging your talented employees and teams. When managers are clear about what's expected and how they interrelate, employees will be too. And this, in turn, will improve trust, comfort, and focus on the most important work (versus worry, tension, and failure to trust).

Shore Up Management Fundamentals from Top to Bottom

In Chapter 1, "Executive Team Execution," we suggested that leadership teams consider measuring their success based on how well they build management team capabilities. If you are concerned about building a positive employees relations environment (and particularly if remaining union-free is an organizational goal), it is important to own this measurement as a team. Before we share our specific recommendations, we need to define what we mean by management fundamentals. Ironically, there is no one list of what managers and supervisors need to know that we feel is adequate to address today's challenges, so it is better to specify what a fundamental is:

> *Management fundamental:* One of the most important skills that managers at this organization needs to be successful.

Let's break that down a bit more. First of all, we need to define managerial success. How do you define success? If you want to build a positive employee relationship environment, then managerial success looks like this:

- Managers are known as being open, warm, caring, and trustworthy.
- Managers are likeable and make even the toughest work fun at times.
- Managers (this includes senior leaders, middle managers, supervisors, and leads) work well together and seem to be

singing from the same song sheet, even if their individual styles are different.

- Managers model great teaming skills.
- Managers are adaptable and nimble and help their employees deal well with changes.
- Managers build interest and commitment in business results. They are result-oriented in ways that engage workers.
- Managers are able to help employees deal with team tension, stress, and differences.
- Managers have the courage to deal with performance problems.
- Managers act consistently where it matters (performance standards, adherence to policies, culture, OT/promotions/pay decisions).
- Managers build ownership through empowerment, enabling employee growth, and offering variety and challenge.
- Managers have the strength and confidence to lead and the humbleness to follow.

This is how we would define managerial success for creating a positive employee relations environment. How does this match up with your thinking? If you evaluated your managers based on these criteria, how many are successful today?

Let's get back to our definition of a management fundamental. If this is how we gauge success, then we can describe the first part of the definition—*one of the most important skills*. The most important skills needed to produce success as we define it above are

- Building relationships
- Managing change
- Adjusting work practices
- Performance management
- Improving employee motivation
- Coaching and supporting employees
- Personal impact and integrity
- Building partnerships

- Likability
- Team building
- How to manage consistently as part of a management team
- Leadership and followership

If you want to shore up management fundamentals, you might want to start with this list and tailor it to your organization's needs. Don't delegate ownership of the management teams' effectiveness to the training or HR departments; building managerial talent is one of your most important responsibilities as a leadership team. And while you might not be conducting training or creating the training plan, you will want to ensure that all managers are equipped and capable and that they are held accountable. We also would encourage you to discuss managerial skills as a team and not delegate it to individual leaders to own because differences in skills across the organization can cause big problems, including perceptions of unequal treatment, favoritism, and lack of trust in management.

While managers of many styles can be successful, there are certain practices that should be applied consistently to create a positive employee relations environment. Extremes (some great managers and some ineffective managers) bring attention to what's lacking in the management system and tend to lower the overall perception of the management team (even for employees who work for the great managers). In addition to the ideas just shared, if you want to create a positive employee relations environment

- Align communication and relationship building practices to strengthen teamwork between layers of management and improve the amount and quality of communication moving up and down the organization.
- Clarify roles for frontline supervision and reinforce them through inclusion in management communication and with how they are evaluated and reinforced. Paint a clear picture for what excellent frontline supervision looks like in action every day.
- Ensure that all managers are effectively trained on and practicing good management fundamentals.

Although we have focused a lot on remaining union-free in this chapter, the practices we recommend are beneficial to organizations that already work with a union and those that don't face that risk. We have worked with senior leadership teams who get shocked into awareness after their organization is targeted by a union. At this point, it is often too late to discover the health of your employee-management relationships and do anything to improve it. We also have worked with clients who believe the famous Ben Franklin quote that "An ounce of prevention is worth a pound of cure." They proactively build relationships at all levels and are visible, assess their organization for vulnerability, seek to understand their connectivity index, and own making sure their managers and supervisors are capable of and motivated to create a positive employee relations environment. Which leadership team do you want to be?

"For it is mutual trust, even more than mutual interest that holds human associations together. Our friends seldom profit us but they make us feel safe... Marriage is a scheme to accomplish exactly that same end."

—H.L. Mencken

Endnotes

1. In Oren Harari, *The Leadership Secrets of Colin Powell*, 19.

2. Seth Godin, *Tribes: We Need You to Lead Us*, 18.

Conclusion: A Manifesto About Love and Leadership

"People are unreasonable, illogical, and self-centered. Love them anyway."
—Mother Teresa

Steve Farber is a best-selling author and a dynamic keynote speaker who talks about leadership. Several months ago, we interviewed Steve for our podcast, and the topic was leadership love. Specifically, we wanted to explore why "love" should be a word we use in conjunction with professional leadership and how leaders should distinguish what it means to demonstrate love at work. Here is a quote from Steve Farber's book, *The Radical Leap*, which echoes some of what we discussed during the podcast:

> Love is the ultimate motivation of the Extreme Leader: love of something or someone; love of a cause; love of a principle; love of the people you work with and the customers you serve; love of the future you and yours can create together; love of the business you conduct together every day.[1]

We believe that the ideas we have shared in this book boil down to love, too, and we hope you have become enamored with the idea that your leadership team is a beautiful vehicle for generating organization growth and success. Leadership team excellence is an inspiring thing to watch in action, and we hope that you will find and enjoy your team's performance sweet spot.

"We shall have to repent in this generation not so much for the evil deeds of the wicked people but for the appalling silence of the good people."
—Martin Luther King

We assume that you are all hard-working, dedicated, and well-meaning professionals because nearly every senior leader we have met has been. This is not enough, however, to propel your team performance to reach your potential. Many leadership teams operate well below their capabilities, and often it is because they have not yet seen and embraced the power of their teams.

You and your peers cannot do your best work unless you tap into your deepest drives, passions, and commitments. Distraction and disconnection plunges our potential into the background where it waits to come alive again.

Why all this talk of love and why now at the end of the book? If you have made it to this conclusion, we have at least captured your attention, and we assume that you have some interest in building leadership team excellence. Through the eight chapters in this book we have shared hundreds of ideas and suggested dozens of beliefs that will serve you and your team. Some of these beliefs we have proposed include

- We are a team, not a collection of individuals.
- What we do is visible and sets the tone for the rest of the organization.
- We need to measure our success so we know if our team processes and practices are working.
- As a team, we need to build strong and support relationships regardless of how we feel about each other's styles. Letting styles clash and get in the way of our collaboration is not acceptable.
- Meetings are money, and our meetings are very expensive. Our team meetings need to meet the hurdle of opportunity costs.
- We need to be known and trusted at all levels of the organization.

- We own building managerial talent and ensuring the organization's bench strength.
- We are the ones who should define the desired culture, model it, and make decisions that move the culture forward.
- To help our organization be agile, we need to be an agile leadership team.
- The senior leadership team plays a very important role in helping the organization remain union-free.

We have offered a lot of ideas, and some of these team adjustments might be large if you and your peers have not thought about how you operate as a team before. What will save you from getting overwhelmed? Love. Leadership is really a job of expressing love, and it is worth all the hard work when we tap into our passion for the work.

"Opportunity is missed by most people because it is dressed in overalls and looks like work."
—Thomas Edison

Yes, we agree that you need to focus on financial results. Love and financial results are not on opposite ends of any spectrum. This is serious business, and only with deep emotion and personal velocity can we create great value and leave a lasting legacy.

Love is the thread that ties every chapter of this book together and, likewise, it is love that brings the best leadership teems together. Love for their business, love for their roles, love for the promise of what a great leadership team can do for an organization. And love for each other—whether you are great pals or peers who aren't drawn to be friends. You need love to make the 5% of your time spent together the most productive. Lesser feelings will yield only mediocre results. The work of a leader is too hard, too demanding, and too draining to be powered by anything but love.

Will You Go for the Gold?

You and your peers have been selected to run things and to succeed. Like an Olympic team, you each possess extraordinary talents. You are world-class and have worked your entire career to reach this position. You know that it is an honor to represent your organization and to serve its mission, and you feel privileged. Is it enough for you that you made it on the team, or do you want to also want to go for the gold? You and your peers need to choose between participating and winning because the paths forward for each are very different. Will yours be a dream team or an assembly of talented individuals who never quite lived up to their collective potential?

"Without the calling and commitment of your heart, there's no good reason for you to take a stand, to take a risk, to do what it takes to change your world for the better."[2]
—Steve Farber

We hope that after reading this book you have a clearer idea of what it means to be a great leadership team and that you and your peers are driven to your best work together. Here's a summary of ways that we suggested that you can bring forth leadership love and maximize your collective impact.

Executive Team Execution

The team is a powerful construct from which you and your peers transform your organization. But do you see it this way, or are you operating as a group of talented individuals who periodically come together to make decisions and create strategic plans? The choice you make is important and will determine how your success ought to be measured. The well-worn adage that one plus one equals three could be updated to read ten leaders, when operating as a well-running team, can have the impact of 100 leaders. We believe the team-premium is that large.

Leaders who commit themselves to be a great team will be best served by measures of success that tell them whether their time is having their intended impact. What are you measuring as a team, and what's most important for you to measure? The leadership team is the compass that determines direction. How will you know if your leadership is pointing in the right direction? Ensuring alignment is not always a straightforward thing. We know many talented leadership teams that are not modeling the culture they seek, for example. Think about the first job you got running a department or division. We would guess that one of the first things you did was to implement performance measures to determine how the department was working and where changes would make the greatest positive difference. You cared about this department and wanted to make it better, right? Apply this same affection, curiosity, and ownership to the effectiveness of your leadership team.

"The greater danger for most of us lies not in setting our aim too high and falling short, but in setting our aim too low, and achieving our mark."

—Michelangelo

The Clash of Titans: Executive Teaming

Who are you together, and does your love, admiration, and support come through in everything you do together and how you represent each other? What? Are you whispering into the book that you do not love your fellow leadership team members? Okay, but let's look at this another way. The team is the team, and unless you are the man or woman on the top of the organization chart, it is not your responsibility to judge leadership team members—it is your job to partner well with each person and be an excellent team member. The goal, by the way, is not simply getting along. As leaders, you want to have a great working relationship. What can you do to build deep and caring partnerships with peers who you might not want to accompany out for after-work drinks or on the golf course? It is important to get to the place where regardless of your differences, you appreciate each other's strengths and support each other's growth. You are important to one another and like tightly bonded military squads, you need to put aside personality or style differences to be great together. Everyone on the leadership team brings to it amazing skills, energy, drive, wisdom, and experience. Find that for each of you and tap into it.

This is the essence of love for the team—being rock solid about your mission and believing and feeling pride in the fact that this is your unit. Everything you do sets the tone for those who look up to you in the organization, which is a humbling burden and a privilege. Great teaming cannot come from disconnected individuals—at any level of the organization. Fall in love with the compelling nature of the team and then with the valued colleagues who are your partners.

Meetings Are Money

Love your time, for it is your most precious resource and tool for leading. Many executives think they value time but are proved wrong when their calendar is put aside their values, mission, top priorities, and most important leadership intentions.

And the meeting has the greatest appetite for time of most any work activity. The more people you put into a room, the greater the multiplier of potential waste, dysfunction, and evaporation of time. Ten-minute breaks turn into 20-minute sliding restarts. Well-intended inclusion slows progress to a snail's pace, and grandstanding meeting participants turn hour-long staff meetings into 90-minute distractions with an aggravating after-taste of time that you will never get back. The costs of meetings are high, and opportunity costs even higher.

Meetings do not have to be weapons of corporate destruction; they can be catalysts for change, tools that enable focus, and vehicles for building work relationships. How? When time is revered as precious. When we love our time and live by the vow to use time to create change, momentum, and connection. Imagine that your hour-long staff meeting was a gift that could catalyze generative thinking that leads to productivity breakthroughs. How might you approach your meetings if you loved them this way? Leadership team meetings are the most expensive, and every moment consumes huge amounts of opportunity lost. Each moment of time is a precious gift and doorway of possibility.

"The speed of a runaway horse counts for nothing."
—Jean Cocteau

Culture Is the Context and Often the Answer

What do you love about your organization? What is it about your workplace that saps you of your energy and drive? The chances are good that both have something to do with the organization's culture. The culture is your context—or the container—from which you create the vibe and characteristics of the workplace. If you love where you work, you will bring love to the work. Great leaders endeavor to build great cultures.

The leadership team gets to create culture, mold it, improve it, and they can also destroy it. You nurture and feed your culture with vision, energy, love, and care, and it will serve your organization's path forward like a clear, fast running river filled with diverse life and nutrients. Without love, the workplace will feel institutional—the path becomes a memo with bullet points and a black binder filled with policies and gunked-up legalese. *Sign here, acknowledging your receipt.* Metal, cement, and paper don't rouse employees' commitment or cause them to share their hearts and minds with you. Uninspired, they will save themselves for their churches, soccer teams, back-yard projects, and side businesses. These parts of our life are important, for sure, but great workplaces earn their share of engaged

and focused performance. When leaders love their organization's culture—when they care for it—they create inspiring spaces that pull
employees and customers in where their energy fertilizes it further.
Strong cultures are beloved places where people can flourish.

---

*"Creativity is not a tangible asset like mineral deposits that can
be hoarded or fought over or even bought and sold. We must
begin to think of creativity as a common good, like liberty or
security. It is something essential that belongs to all of us, and
that must always be fed, renewed and maintained—or else it
will slip away."*[3]
—Richard Florida

They Are All Moments of Truth

We like to produce charts with boxes and arrows that tell us how
things are going and where our work processes can be improved. The
most important parts of these charts are often not talked about, however. The boxes might tell you the task that person A is to complete,
but the arrow between the boxes indicates the necessity of a relationship between A and B. It is the arrows that are most important for
they represent how people are connected.

Leaders are leaders of people, not things, and people follow men
and women who they feel they know and can trust. Effective leaders
place a high value on getting to know employees at all levels of the
organization. When you are a busy executive, however, this may be
hard to do and fit into your day. You could read a few books and go to
a seminar to learn the skills you need for speaking, listening, and
introducing yourself to employees at the summer picnic, but these
skills will not create connection and not quickly enough given your
job's demands. But love can. In fact, only love can reach into your
employees' hearts and minds fast and directly like a laser beam. An
executive with highly flawed presentation skills but a strong and
warm heart will be much more highly regarded than a polished and

practiced professional who fails to share of himself with authenticity. Employees will feel they know and can trust the leadership team when its members—who may come across with differing styles—all reach employees with openness and authenticity. The opportunity to connect is an honor, and we invite you to fall in love with the idea of high visibility everywhere in the organization.

"Motivating with fear and influencing with bribery are felonies. They are toxic and unprincipled. They are haunting human cultural hangovers from slavery bondage, and serfdom. They are not leadership any more than a great white shark in a splash pool is a canned tuna."[4]

—Gus Lee

Getting Better Together

Have you embraced the belief that your strengths and weaknesses are known and that we are all beautifully flawed professionals? This is a belief that can turn self-doubt into humble but confident self-confidence. Senior leaders receive much less feedback about the efficacy of their styles and methods even though their decisions and actions impact people and the business more than when they were middle managers and supervisors.

Leaders do not give up their human drives when they get promoted to the corner office. They, like all employees, are intrinsically motivated by growth, progress, and challenge. And for senior leaders, the stakes are higher, making their development more critical. How in tune with your strengths and weaknesses are you? Are you aware of potential fatal flaws that could derail your career and cause problems throughout the organization? Self-awareness is a gift—embrace it.

Growth is enlivening, and leadership team members are in the best position to support each other's development. Imagine the impact that a team event will have when you learn cutting edge theories that could revolutionize your business. Doing this together will speed up how and whether learning is used to improve results. And imagine the closeness you will feel when you support each other's personal development goals. You can use the bonds created during peer coaching and for day-to-day collaboration, partnership, and problem solving. Great leadership team learning requires a love of bettering your capabilities and being authentically self-aware.

"Only by choosing activities in the learning zone can one make progress. That's the location of skills and abilities that are just out of reach. We can never make progress in the comfort zone because those are the activities we can already do easily, while panic-zone activities are so hard that we don't even know how to approach them."[5]

—Geoff Colvin

Creating an Agile Organization

Imagine a crowd on the dance floor. They change their moves—speed, direction, size of their gestures—with each song. They accommodate people coming on and off the floor and have a good sense of what's going on around them. They don't attempt slow-dance moves during upbeat songs. Most people have their own dance moves and styles, but their heads and feet still move in concert. There is joy in listening, being moved, and then moving in rhythm with the music.

Corporate agility is like this dance scene. When we are nimble, we adjust based on the cadence, and we do so with joy and acceptance. Don't look at being agile as a chore or a new skill to conquer because it is a way of working more than anything. Agility is work, yes, but not something that requires a certification or complicated charts and graphs. It can be enhanced with simple questions like, "Are there ways in which we should revisit how we are doing things?"

Leadership teams can create a nimble workplace or reinforce a rigid one. Which will you and your peers advocate? Agility is a goal that is important for the team to share and consistently apply because variations in adaptability cause friction and dysfunction between teams. When you improve organizational agility, your teams do work that is more relevant and will experience less change-related stress. Do you love results more than the comfort of your ingrained habits? Tap into your desire to have a positive impact and to collaborate with your peers on ways the leadership team can best model nimbleness. Love the nature of the dance floor.

"Dance is the only art of which we ourselves are the stuff of which it is made."
—Ted Shawn

Leadership Team Strategies for Remaining Union-Free

There is perhaps no clearer place where leadership love is needed, appreciated, and makes an impact than in establishing a positive employee relations environment. It is not enough that people feel you have treated them fairly. They want to be treated with love. They want to know that you care and that their work—even the most rudimentary task—is important and makes a difference.

You might see the goal of making workers feel valued and important as part of the supervisor's job description. And you would be right. And you might say that it is a fundamental job responsibility that all leaders create a connecting and warm workplace where employees trust your words and respect you. And you would be right. And if you also said that an important part of the senior leader's role is to be known, trusted, and liked by employees at all levels, you would also be right. There are many tasks where delegation is critical to getting it all done, but be wary of overdelegating relationship building with frontline employees. While you cannot spend hours with each employee, it is important that they feel connected to you. And it is important that as a team, you have developed a reputation for being open, friendly, trustworthy, and inspiring. When your employees follow you willingly, you will receive their gifts of engagement and ownership. It will take love—love of connection, love of small and special moments—to create a great employee relations environment.

"Push is seductive. It creates the illusion of great power in an era when power is shifting. It can delude organizational leaders into thinking they need only roll out the new plan and massively detailed organizational blueprints will become the new scripts that everyone will surely follow. But this view assumes that individuals are still awaiting their instructions from above... Fewer and fewer of us match that description."[6]

—John Hagel, et al.

What stand will you take as a team? Do you see what's possible? Imagine if this were a typical staff meeting:

As you and your fellow team members walk into the meeting room, you greet each other warmly. You shake hands in the same way best friends embrace. The energy is positive, and you dig into the meeting agenda on time. Your conversation is open, and your mutual respect for one another is obvious. Questions are provocative and catalytic—they help move your thinking forward. While you often don't agree with each other, your different approaches and styles make you better leaders. Neither you nor your peers allow differences to become clashes in style. As a team, you reflect on decisions and talk candidly about what's working and not working about your team processes. Courage is rewarded. You make decisions with strategies, values, and your mission in mind. A fly on the wall would report that your conversations are focused and results-oriented. You demonstrate a sense of urgency for what's most important—not a false sense of urgency or frenetic energy. Your staff meetings are excellent examples of conversations that move work forward, build relationships, and provide clear and compelling direction. You care about your team's reputation and feel proud that you and your peers model the desired culture.

If your leadership team staff meeting looked and felt like this, would you love your work a little bit more? The possibility of leadership team excellence is compelling to think about, don't you agree? As a pack of top dogs, team members bring experience, drive, and baggage to the team. And when you use the experience, tap into the drive, and redirect and reduce baggage and learn new skills, you accomplish the very best work that a team can do.

"Happiness is really just about four things: perceived control, perceived progress, connectedness (number and depth of your relationships), and vision/meaning (being a part of something bigger than yourself)."[7]

—Tony Hsieh

Endnotes

1. Steve Farber, *The Radical Leap: A Personal Lesson in Extreme Leadership*, 165.

2. Ibid.

3. Richard Florida, *The Rise of the Creative Class: And How It's Transforming Work, Leisure, Community, and Everyday Life*, xxvi.

4. Gus Lee, *Courage: The Backbone of Leadership*, 122.

5. Geoff Colvin, *Talent Is Overrated: What Really Separates World-Class Performers from Everybody Else*, 68.

6. John Hagel III, John Seely Brown, and Lang Davison, *The Power of Pull: How Small Moves, Smartly Made, Can Set Big Things in Motion*, 183.

7. Tony Hsieh, *Delivering Happiness: A Path to Profits, Passion, and Purpose*, 232.

Appendix: The Leadership Team Excellence Assessment

"The answer is no until you ask the question."
—Mark Tidwell

Throughout this book, we have referred to the Senior Leadership Team Survey we conducted in 2009. We've created a focused set of ten questions that you and your team can explore based on the questions we asked and what we learned from the results. The survey assesses three aspects of team performance including how the team measures success, how the team spends time, and how the team can best impact organizational excellence. We recommend that you and your team use these questions to explore your current practices and create a focused plan for continuous team development and improvement. The 10 questions are listed here and are followed by discussion of each question and interpretation of various results.

The Leadership Team Survey

The following questions will help you self-assess your team's strengths and self-diagnose areas where improvement might make the greatest difference.

Part 1: How We Measure Success

1. How should we measure our success as a *team*? Which of the following should we consider indicators of our success as a leadership team?

   ☐ Financial performance

   ☐ Employee satisfaction

   ☐ Employee retention

   ☐ Customer service

   ☐ Safety

   ☐ Success of decisions made

   ☐ Team cohesion

   ☐ Strength of team relationships

   ☐ Quality

   ☐ Completion of major initiatives

   ☐ Strategic implementation

   ☐ The team's reputation within the organization

   ☐ The team's reputation with customers or stakeholders

   ☐ Relationships built at all levels of the organization

   ☐ Bench strength and succession planning

   ☐ Organizational culture

   ☐ Organizational agility

   ☐ Others: _____

2. How would I characterize our current business results for the following performance indicators? (Exceeding, Meeting, or Not meeting expectations)

	Exceeding expectations	Meeting expectations	Not meeting expectations
Performance to our business plan			
Health of our culture			
Strength of our teams and capabilities			
Quality of our work			

Part 2: How We Spend Time Together

3. Indicate the frequency that our leadership team should engage in the following activities.

   _____ Leadership team meetings

   _____ "Town hall" type meetings

   _____ Joint written communication to employees

   _____ Strategic planning sessions

   _____ Budgeting sessions

   _____ Idea generation

   _____ Representing each other at events training sessions or retreats

   _____ Recreational activities

   _____ Celebration events

   _____ Team performance evaluation discussions

   _____ Joint learning events, peer coaching, other team development

   _____ Informal relationship building gatherings

4. Select the statement that best matches our current involvement in shaping our organizational culture.

   _____ We regularly talk about the organization's culture and believe it is strong and aligned with our strategies.

   _____ We regularly discuss how the organization's culture ought to change and put practices in place to facilitate its change.

   _____ We have talked about the organization's culture, believe it should change, but have not done anything to change it.

   _____ We have not talked about the organization's culture in the last year.

5. Imagine there is a fly on the wall listening to our leadership team conversations and observing how we interact with one another. Indicate what the fly is likely to see, hear, and conclude.

	Very visible/ evident	Somewhat visible/ evident	The fly won't see this
Team members are candid with each other.			
Team members respect each other.			
Team members like each other.			
Each team member is qualified and a good fit for the team.			
Each team member pulls his or her weight.			
All team members are engaged and proactive.			
Meetings are well-run and productive.			
Team members look out for each other and don't let each other fail.			
Team members share the same priorities.			
Leadership styles sometimes clash within the team.			
The team makes effective decisions together.			
The team regularly engages in healthy debate.			
The team is focused on what matters most.			
Team members possess positive executive presence.			
Team members seem nimble and flexible.			
Team members prepare well for team meetings.			

	Very visible/ evident	Somewhat visible/ evident	The fly won't see this
Team members represent each other well.			
The team is results-oriented and gets things done.			
The team looks for and reduces barriers to success.			
The team is willing to rethink strategies or ideas that are no longer the right choice.			
The team is willing to take risks after careful consideration of the pros and cons.			

6. This team acts more like a collection of individuals versus a team with common goals and measures of success.

   _____ True

   _____ False

7. Which of the following executive skills would you like to further develop in the next two years? (Check all that apply.)

   ☐ Financial analysis

   ☐ Coaching others

   ☐ Strategic thinking

   ☐ Business development

   ☐ Planning

   ☐ Time management for executives

   ☐ Building strategic relationships

   ☐ Executive influence

   ☐ Change leadership

   ☐ Presentation skills

   ☐ Organizational alignment

☐   Organizational culture development

☐   Results orientation and discipline

☐   Executive teaming

☐   Other (please specify)_____

Part 3: How We Impact Organizational Excellence

8. Select the statement that best characterizes how our organization views us, as a leadership team.

____ This leadership team is known by and enjoys a positive reputation at all levels of the organization.

____ This leadership team is most visible to the middle management ranks. We rarely communicate with supervisors and frontline employees.

____ Our organization cascades communication, so only the next level or two below us will feel like they know us.

9. Which aspects of organizational performance most need our attention?

☐   Our culture

☐   Building a positive employee relations environment

☐   Modeling the values, mission, and desired culture

☐   Building organizational agility

☐   Building talent, bench strength, and succession

☐   Building and modeling effective meeting skills

☐   Our development as a team

☐   Connectivity index, building positive relationships

☐   Building results orientation, growing the business

10. How engaged are we as a team? Is our passion and commitment for the business obvious to each other, our managers, and our employees?

_____

_____

_____

_____

_____

_____

The Leadership Team Survey with Discussion Notes

Part 1: How We Measure Success

The questions in Part 1 should help you and your team explore, narrow down, and agree on a focused set of measures for your team. You might find that some people are hesitant to discuss team measures, perhaps because they are not sold on the idea of having specific measures for the team. If you get the sense that some of your peers might feel this way, be sure to initiate an open conversation about this. Moving from an individual leader mindset to a team mindset might take time and discussion, but it is the right conversation to have and could immediately refocus your team. Most of the teams we have surveyed and worked with have started with some level of disagreement about whether team measures were of value. Embedded in this disagreement are differences of opinion about whether the team is really a team.

1. How should we measure our success as a *team*? Which of the following should we consider indicators of our success as a leadership team?

   The goal here is not to pick them all. In fact, you want to use this question to begin the process of selecting a short list of measures that will make the greatest difference to improving team performance. Use the information found in Chapter 1, "Executive Team Execution," to support this discussion. We like using the long list to give leaders ideas. If we asked this question without offering the list, it is likely that many of these indicators would never be considered.

2. How would I characterize our current business results for the following performance indicators? (Exceeding, Meeting, or Not meeting expectations)

You might be surprised at the level of disagreement within the team about current results—and not just in the fuzzy people areas! When we conducted our survey, we asked participants to rate their current level of business results (bottom line results) as a demographic that we could use to cut the data by results. What we found, however, is that there was rarely agreement about current results within the leadership team. It is good to know how each leadership team member would assess results because whatever they feel is being transmitted to the managers and team that report to them. If you are communicating that things are going great and your peer is communicating that things are not going great, this will cause tension, stress, and poor focus throughout the organization. The senior team ought to agree on the answers to this question, and the discussion that this survey item provokes might help your team improve their level of agreement.

Part 2: How We Spend Time Together

This section of the survey is designed to catalyze team discussion about how you spend the precious 5% of your time together. The options listed here offer options that you can use to select ways to improve the effectiveness of your team activities. The goal is not to select more activities, but to select better ways to spend time together.

3. Indicate the frequency that our leadership team should engage in the following activities.

We like this list of options and encourage you and your team to consider the value of activities beyond staff meetings and strategic planning and budgeting discussions. Your team should spend some time collectively communicating with the people in the organization and should spend some time building your team relationships and skills.

4. Select the statement that best matches our current involvement in shaping our organizational culture.

   As mentioned in Chapter 4, "Culture Is the Context and Often the Answer," we found that leadership team members had very different views about what their team has discussed about culture and what they've done to improve it. Interestingly, we found the greatest level of variability in this survey item within the teams that said they measured their success in ways that they really don't. We are not suggesting that these leaders were untruthful. We think, and follow-up discussions support, that they think they are more proactive as a team than they really are.

5. Imagine there is a fly on the wall listening to our leadership team conversations and observing how we interact with one another. Indicate what the fly is likely to see, hear, and conclude. (Very visible/evident, Somewhat visible/evident, The fly won't see this)

   We love this survey item! If you can, give team members the options to select their responses anonymously before you discuss the results. Depending on the level of dysfunction within your team, team members might not feel comfortable being the first person to verbalize that styles clash within the team or that some team members do not prepare for meetings.

6. This team acts more like a collection of individuals versus a team with common goals and measures of success. (True or False)

   The answer to this item should not be viewed as bad or good. If your team has been operating as a collection of individuals, that is fine. Don't make this wrong but discuss what might be possible if you also worked more as a team. Focus on the current and future—what's possible—not on the past and whether you have been doing the right things in the right ways. As we mentioned in Chapter 1, it is not at all uncommon for leadership teams to operate as collections of individuals.

7. Which of the following executive skills would you like to further develop in the next two years? (Check all that apply.)

   Although we encourage team members to check every topic that they believe would be of benefit, the goal is not to come up with a long list of to-dos. You want to discover the one or two topics that many team members are interested in learning more about so that you can plan some development activities as a team. We also like using this long list because it will give you and your peers ideas that support many of the ideas presented in this book. So if we have piqued your interest in how your team can improve, you might want to turn that into team development efforts.

Part 3: How We Impact Organizational Excellence

The purpose of this section of the survey is to help your team explore and plan how you want to most impact the organization over the next year or two. Be open about the current reality and focus on what's possible and the outcomes that would most enliven organizational success and results.

8. Select the statement that best characterizes how our organization views us, as a leadership team.

   This is probably one of the toughest items on this survey. You might want to refer to your most recent employee engagement survey to get clues about how the organization views your team and the reputation you have built (and how it might differ among managers and frontline employees). One team we surveyed also happened to be a client of our engagement survey services. While frontline employees rated their leadership team as somewhat disconnected and ineffective, the leadership team gave their reputation higher marks. Use whatever data you have within your organization, combined with good observation, to understand your impact on others. You might also want to ask your management team to tell you how they would assess your reputation and what they think the frontline employees say about the leadership team. Whatever the situation (good, bad, or ugly), you want to know. You don't want to be the last to know.

9. Which aspects of organizational performance most need our attention?

   This survey item should lead to great discussion, and we recommend that you discuss this before creating your strategic plan. Make sure that your strategic plan addresses those areas that the team agrees should be top priorities and where their impact would make the greatest difference. Use this topic to reenergize the team's passion for improving the business.

10. How engaged are we as a team? Is our passion and commitment for the business obvious to each other, our managers, and our employees?

    Not every team will be able to have a candid conversation about this, but try. If you believe that you can expect your managers and employees to be as committed, engaged, and passionate about their work as you are and demonstrate (we do!), then this might be the most important item on this survey. If it will help you and your peers open up, change the question to be less threatening like, "In what ways can we demonstrate our passion and commitment for the business?"

The Leadership Team Survey as a Tool for Development

When we surveyed teams, we noticed an interesting trend that helped us realize that the survey itself was a tool for development. Learning starts when how we think changes, when we are provoked, and when we explore new ideas. Several of these survey items will seem curious to some of you and your peers and may get the wheels turning in your head. Survey participants told us that the questions left them thinking about leadership team excellence in different ways, and this is excellent. So consider using this survey as both a feedback tool and a development activity.

"You can observe a lot just by watching."
—Yogi Berra

References

Appelbaum, L., and M. Paese. "What Senior Leaders Do: The Nine Roles of Strategic Leadership." DDI White Paper, 2008.

Avrin, David. *It's Not Who You Know—It's Who Knows You!: The Small Business Guide to Raising Your Profits by Raising Your Profile*. Hoboken, NJ: Wiley, 2009.

Bock, Wally. "Can Leadership Be Taught?" October 13, 2009.http://blog. threestarleadership.com/2009/10/13/can-leadership-be-taught.aspx.

Bolt, J., M. McGrath, and M. Dulworth. *Strategic Executive Development: The Five Essential Investments*. San Francisco: Pfeiffer, 2005.

Branham, Leigh, and Mark Hirschfeld. *Re-Engage: How America's Best Places to Work Inspire Extra Effort in Extraordinary Times*. New York: McGraw-Hill, 2010.

Bryant, John Hope. *Love Leadership: The New Way to Lead in a Fear-Based World*. San Francisco: Jossey Bass, 2009.

Bunker, K., D. Hall, and K. Kram. *Extraordinary Leadership: Addressing the Gaps in Senior Executive Development*. San Francisco: Jossey Bass, 2010.

Carlzon, Jan. *Moments of Truth*. New York: Harper Paperbacks, 1989.

Cialdini, Robert B. *Influence: Science and Practice*. Prentice Hall, 2008.

Cohen, Aubrey. "Pilot Sullenberger spins life lessons from Hudson landing." *Seattle PI* blog, March 8, 2010. http://blog.seattlepi.com/aerospace/archives/197075.asp.

Colvin, Geoffrey. *Talent Is Overrated: What Really Separates World-Class Performers from Everybody Else*. New York: Penguin Group, 2008.

Covey, Stephen M.R. *The Speed of Trust: The One Thing That Changes Everything.* New York: Free Press, 2006.

Csikszentmihalyi, Mihaly. *Good Business: Leadership, Flow, and the Making of Meaning.* New York: Penguin Group, 2005.

Deal, Terrence, and Allan Kennedy. *Corporate Cultures.* Reading, MA: Addison-Wesley Publishing, 1982.

Dixon, Patrick. *Futurewise: Six Faces of Global Change.* London: Profile Books, 2007.

Drucker, Peter F. *The Effective Executive.* New York: Harper & Rom, 1967.

———. *Managing the Non-Profit Organization: Practices and Principles.* New York: HarperBusiness, 1992.

Farber, Steve. *The Radical Leap: A Personal Lesson in Extreme Leadership.* Chicago: Kaplan Publishing, 2009.

Ferrazzi, Keith. *Never Eat Alone: And Other Secrets to Success, One Relationship at a Time.* Crown Business, 2005.

Firestein, Peter. *Crisis of Character: Building Corporate Reputation in the Age of Skepticism.* Union Square Press, 2009.

Florida, Richard. *The Rise of the Creative Class: And How It's Transforming Work, Leisure, Community, and Everyday Life.* New York: Basic Books, 2003.

Ford, Jeffrey, and Laurie Ford. *The Four Conversations: Daily Communication That Gets Results.* San Francisco: Berrett-Koehler Publishers, 2009.

Gebelein, S., D. Lee, K. Nelson-Neuhaus, and E. Sloan. *Successful Executive's Handbook.* Minneapolis: Personnel Decisions International, 1999.

Godin, Seth. *Tribes: We Need You to Lead Us.* New York: Portfolio, 2008.

Goldman, Steven, Roger Nagel, and Kenneth Preiss. *Agile Competitors and Virtual Organizations: Strategies for Enriching the Customer.* New York: Van Nostrand Reinhold Press, 1995.

Goldsmith, Marshall. "Try Feedforward Instead of Feedback." 2002. www.marshallgoldsmithlibrary.com/cim/articles_display.php?aid=110.

———. *What Got You Here, Won't Get You There.* New York: Hyperion, 2007.

Grantham, Charles, James Ware, and Cory Williamson. *Corporate Agility: A Revolutionary New Model for Competing in a Flat World*. New York: Amacom Press, 2007.

Hagel, John, III, John Seely Brown, and Lang Davison. *The Power of Pull: How Small Moves, Smartly Made, Can Set Big Things in Motion*. New York: Basic Books, 2010.

Harari, Oren. *The Leadership Secrets of Colin Powell*. New York: McGraw-Hill, 2002.

Hofstede, Geert. *Culture's Consequences*. Newbury Park, CA: Sage Publications, 1980.

Hsieh, Tony. *Delivering Happiness: A Path to Profits, Passion, and Purpose*. New York: Business Plus, 2010.

———. "On a Scale of 1 to 10, How Weird Are You?" *The New York Times*, January 9, 2010. www.nytimes.com/2010/01/10/business/10corner.html.

Jarski, Rosemarie. *Words from the Wise: Over 6,000 of the Smartest Things Ever Said*. New York: Skyhorse Publishing, 2007.

Jensen, Bill, and Josh Klein. "The HBR List: Breakthrough Ideas for 2010." *Harvard Business Review*, January–February 2010.

Kopeikina, Luda. *The Right Decision Every Time: How to Reach Perfect Clarity on Tough Decisions*. Upper Saddle River, NJ: Prentice Hall, 2005.

Kotter, John P. *Leading Change*. Boston: Harvard Business Press, 1996.

———. *A Sense of Urgency*. Boston: Harvard Business Press, 2008.

———, and James Heskett. *Corporate Culture and Performance*. New York: The Free Press, 1992.

Lee, Gus. *Courage: The Backbone of Leadership*. San Francisco: Jossey Bass, 2006.

Longenecker, Papp, and Stansfield. "Quarterbacking Real and Rapid Organizational Improvement." *Leader to Leader Institute*, Winter 2009.

Louis, Meryl Reis. "Organizations as Culture-Bearing Milieux." In *Organizational Symbolism*, L.R. Pondy, et al., ed. Greenwich, CT: JAI Press, 1983.

Maira, Arun, and Peter Scott-Morgan. *The Accelerating Organization: Embracing the Human Face of Change*. New York: McGraw-Hill, 1997.

McCann, Selsky, and Lee. "Building Agility, Resilience, and Performance in Turbulent Environments." *People and Strategy* (2009), Issue 3.

McKee, Steve. "Don't Neglect Internal Branding." *BusinessWeek,* December 11, 2009. www.businessweek.com/smallbiz/content/dec2009/sb20091210_167541.htm.

Melancon, Dwayne. "How do you carry the load?" January 26, 2010. http://genuinecuriosity.com/genuinecuriosity/2010/1/26/how-do-you-carry-the-load.html.

Morgan, Howard, Phil Harkins, and Marshall Goldsmith, ed. *The Art and Practice of Leadership Coaching: 50 Top Executive Coaches Reveal Their Secrets.* New York: John Wiley and Sons, 2005.

Pal, Nirmal, and Daniel Pantaleo. *The Agile Enterprise: Reinventing Your Organization for Success in an On-Demand World.* New York: Springer, 2005.

Peters, Tom. *The Little Big Things: 163 Ways to Pursue Excellence.* New York: HarperBusiness, 2010.

————. "Rule #3: Leadership Is Confusing as Hell." February 28, 2001. www.fastcompany.com/magazine/44/rules.html?page=0%2C1.

Schein, Edgar H. *Organization Culture and Leadership.* San Francisco: Jossey Bass, 1985.

Schwartz, Tony. "The CEO Is the Chief Energy Officer." *A Better Way of Working* blog, June 2, 2010. www.theenergyproject.com/blog/ceo-chief-energy-officer.

————. *The Way We're Working Isn't Working: The Four Forgotten Needs That Energize Great Performance.* New York: Free Press, 2010.

Schwarz, Roger. *The Skilled Facilitator: A Comprehensive Resource for Consultants, Facilitators, Managers, Trainers, and Coaches.* San Francisco: Jossey Bass, 2002.

Siehl, Caren, and Joanne Martin. "The Role of Symbolic Management: How Can Managers Effectively Transmit Organizational Culture?" In *Leaders and Managers: International Perspectives on Managerial Behavior and Leadership,* James G. Hunt, et al. Elsevier Science & Technology Books, 1984.

Starbucker, Terry. "Leadership: The Musical." July 5, 2007. www.terrystarbucker.com/2007/07/05/leadership-the-musical/.

Strickland, Bill. *Make the Impossible Possible: One Man's Crusade to Inspire Others to Dream Bigger and Achieve the Extraordinary.* New York: Doubleday, 2007.

Tapomoy, Deb. *A Conceptual Approach to Strategic Talent Management.* Indus Publishing, 2005.

Thiry, Kent. "What a Values-Based Turnaround Looks Like." *Chief Executive*, May/June 2009. www.chiefexecutive.net/ME2/Audiences/dirmod. asp?sid=&nm=&type=Publishing&mod=Publications%3A%3AArticle& mid=8F3A7027421841978F18BE895F87F791&tier=4&id=40203A7A21E A4E83A4C4052D028D75C7&AudID=AE720E7DE3FE473693930869A 5157C27.

Trompenaars, Fons. *Riding the Waves of Culture: Understanding Diversity in Global Business.* London: The Economist Books, 1993.

Unrich, D., N. Smallwood, and K. Sweetman. *The Leadership Code: Five Rules to Lead By*. Boston: Harvard Business Press, 2008.

Widdows, Peter. "Changing a Losing Culture." *CEO Forum Group*, May 2004. www.ceoforum.com.au/article-detail.cfm?cid=6280&t=/Peter-Widdows—Heinz-Australia/Changing-a-Losing-Culture/.

Zenger, John, and Joseph Folkman. *The Extraordinary Leader: Turning Good Managers into Great Leaders.* New York: McGraw-Hill, 2002.

About the Authors

Jim Taylor and Lisa Haneberg share a passion for helping leaders do their best work through practices, actions, habits, and a vision that catalyzes organizational success. Both Jim and Lisa have been exploring the keys to senior leader effectiveness their entire careers.

Jim Taylor is President and CEO of MPI Consulting. A seasoned business and consulting executive with over three decades of experience, he leads MPI's strategic direction and operations, and guides a team of consulting experts and professionals, ensuring their integrity and accountability for successful client engagement and relationships.

Prior to becoming a consultant, Jim was a healthcare executive for 13 years, serving on two senior leadership teams. He has walked the walk, learned from the best, and observed team practices that have not worked. Jim has also held leadership positions and served on committees with local, state, and national organizations. These organizations include the American Society for Healthcare Human Resources Administration, Bureau of National Affairs, Greater Cincinnati Chamber of Commerce, Greater Cincinnati Health Council, Ohio Society of Hospital Human Resources Administrators, Society for Human Resources Management, and Voluntary Hospitals of America, Inc. Jim holds a master's degree in Business Administration and a bachelor of science in Business Administration.

Jim is a nationally recognized expert in leadership, human resources, and employee/labor relations and is a frequent speaker, publisher, and quoted expert on issues surrounding leadership, organizational performance, and positive employee relations. Jim lives with his lovely wife of 38 years in Cincinnati and has two sons who have followed in his footsteps and who serve on leadership teams of major corporations.

Lisa Haneberg is a Vice President with MPI Consulting where she leads the firm's organizational development (OD) practice. She has more than 25 years of experience with OD consulting, executive development, as well as training and coaching solutions for large and small companies, and government and nonprofit organizations. She has particular expertise in the areas of talent management, succession planning, organizational agility and alignment, middle management effectiveness and development, senior team development, and executive coaching.

Prior to joining MPI, Lisa ran a successful consulting practice and held internal leadership positions in several Fortune 500 companies. She has worked in and with organizations such as Black & Decker, Mead Paper, Intel, Amazon.com, Corbis, MTD Products, Perfetti vanMelle, TUI Travel International, Royal Thai Government, the FAA, the EPA, Microsoft, and the City of Seattle. She holds a bachelor of science degree in Behavioral Sciences from the University of Maryland and holds a master's degree in Fine Arts from Goddard College. In addition, she did graduate studies in Industrial Psychology at Ohio State University and Human Resources and International Business at Johns Hopkins University.

Lisa has published many books about her models and approaches to coaching, management, and leadership. Her book titles include

- *Organization Development Basics* (ASTD Press, 2005)
- *Coaching Basics* (ASTD Press, 2006)
- *Focus Like a Laser Beam: 10 Ways to Do What Matters Most* (Jossey Bass, 2006)
- *Two Weeks to a Breakthrough: How to Zoom Toward Your Goal in 14 Days or Less* (Jossey Bass, 2007)
- *10 Steps to Be a Successful Manager* (ASTD Press, 2007)
- *Developing Great Managers: 20 Power Hours* (ASTD Press, 2008)
- *Hip and Sage: Staying Smart, Cool and Competitive in the Workplace* (Davies Black, 2009)

- *The High Impact Middle Manager: Powerful Strategies to Thrive in the Middle* (ASTD Press, 2010)
- *High Impact Middle Management: Solutions for Today's Busy Public-Sector Managers* (ASTD Press, 2010)
- *Coaching Up and Down the Generations* (ASTD Press, 2010)

In addition, her work has been highlighted in publications such as *Leader to Leader, Washington CEO, Capital,* and *Leadership Excellence.* Lisa is a nationally recognized thought leader in the areas of management and leadership and is called on to speak at private company events and national and regional professional organization conferences. Please go to www.lisahaneberg.com to learn more or visit her Management Craft blog at www.managementcraft.com.

About MPI Consulting

MPI Consulting has been a well-respected niche management consulting firm headquartered in Cincinnati, Ohio, for 36 years. It serves hundreds of clients/corporations and works with thousands of leaders each year. MPI works in three major service areas including

- Labor Relations (including union avoidance work)
- Organization Development (including leadership and management development, talent management, and employee engagement surveys)
- Compensation

MPI offers comprehensive support for leaders in many industries including health care, government, nonprofit, manufacturing, service organizations, and high tech. Since 1974, organizations across the United States have relied on MPI to provide client-centric human resource management consulting services to help them succeed. They help clients in a variety of market sectors define organizational and human resource strategies, as well as design and deploy programs that help them meet their operational objectives. MPI brings integrity, innovation, and execution to every client engagement and relationship.

As relationship builders and thought leaders, the professionals at MPI share what they learn and continually observe how the workplace is changing. As leadership consultants they endeavor to walk their talk and model the behaviors they recommend to clients. They communicate openly, clearly, and in the fashion each client desires, as well as listen, educate, and collaboratively advise so that their clients are the clear engagement owners. MPI's clients are empowered to not only better manage programs and plans going forward, but also to become more solidly rooted as a business partner in their own organizations.

Index